Homeschool Mama Self-Care: Nurturing the Nurturer

Teresa L. Wiedrick
Capturing the Charmed Life

The information in this book is not intended to take the place of qualified medical advice. Please consult your physician or natural health care practitioner before implementing any of the medical ideas in this book.

Dedication

To the ones from whom I learned about
learning:
my homeschooled kids,
Hannah, Madelyn, Rachel & Zachary

To my nurturers and my encouragers,
Jim, Marianna & my mama, Patricia

To my co-travelers,
those homeschool mamas
who are choosing
to thrive, not just survive,

You got this, girlfriends!

"Clearly, Teresa writes from years of valuable experience, and so generously shares them with new homeschool mommas for their benefit. If you're trying to figure out how to get started taking the stress out of your homeschool day, the section where she shares her own story of overwhelm is pure gold! (p116) You'll find solid, experience-tested examples from her own life on creating an environment that is conducive to real education. Also, take note of the authors she recommends as her influencers. If you have to pick a section to start somewhere, there it is! (p 147)"

-Pat Fenner, BreakthroughHomeschooling.com

"I so appreciated your honesty, your humour and your down-to-earth suggestions and ideas. Everything you wrote about felt doable, even with the practicalities of running a household. Such important messages and so well-delivered! A must read..."

-Tamara Strijack, Academic Dean, Neufeld Institute

Contents

HEY MAMA, CAN I TELL YOU WHY I'M HERE?

You don't have to meet me to know I don't have my self-care practices honed to a science, but when you do meet me, you will know for sure. I've only recently taken up running. I eat potato chips with shameful regularity. I tend to pack more activities into my day than I can peacefully enjoy. I am known to make my kids late to extracurriculars as I try to cross stuff off my to-do list. I have argued with my husband in front of the kids. I am still learning not to lose my marbles if more than three kids bicker or loudly complain in a short period.

I am a writing homeschooling mama of four with more than a decade of homeschool experience and a lifetime of writing practice. When I revisit the themes I have most often written about in the last decade, self-care is one of the most common: how to look after myself, keep my sanity, consider my needs, and deal with my emotions as I take care of my family.

Having tried every homeschool philosophy, many curriculums, various ways to menu plan, and different ways to parent, I learned there is no one right way to do any of it. Within three years of homeschooling, I realized that I was exhausted and done. I would have sent my beautiful children to school through the postal system

> Within three years of homeschooling, I realized that I was exhausted and done.

if I could have (I most definitely threatened to do so).

I have been there done that at least twice. Though I would like to blame it on the job, because we all know this is a demanding job, I know I can't. I am responsible to take care of my own needs.

Non-homeschoolers frequently ask homeschool mamas about their kids' socialization. Curiously, homeschool mamas often talk amongst themselves about fulfilling academic requirements. Both of those topics need a discussion, but we should be most concerned with our well-being first. We tend to see the needs outside us rather than inside us. We take on a significant role in our children's lives, usually willingly, and when we do, we need to acknowledge our own needs too.

When parents, in passing, discover I'm a homeschool mama, their jaws have dropped. One person even bowed, but most mamas declare, "I couldn't do that." We know that some days those parents are right: some days we can't homeschool either because some days, it's a lot. Yet, I tend to respond by touting the benefits of this freedom-based lifestyle instead of discussing its challenges.

The general public intuitively knows what we homeschool mamas know after months or years in the trenches; homeschooling is hard work. It's hard work in the organization, coordination, observation, planning, engaging our children well, and as a pure afterthought, caring for our own well-being.

We have more kids than time, more driving time than treadmill time, more dishes to wash than homeschool friends, and more books to purchase than monthly income.

This homeschool mama role is a gratifying one. One that reaps its tiny, though frequent rewards while we're doing it, but a role that secures significant rewards later.

The benefits to this lifestyle are numerous. We chose to homeschool because of the socialization benefit, the congruency with our values, the scheduling freedom, the personalized academic choices, the ability to pursue the rhythm and focus of our life on our own terms. There are reams of reasons why we're doing it.

This book is intended to clarify and encourage you in your self-care practices before you begin homeschooling. This book is intended to help you see through some of your challenges with rose-coloured glasses, instead of the smoky glasses you may have developed over the years. This book is intended to infuse you with the courage to continue homeschooling. And it is intended to encourage you in your self-care practices so you will have the energy and mental clarity to fully engage your children and enjoy the process.

Carpe homeschoolem!

ACKNOWLEDGE YOUR HOMESCHOOL REALITIES

The first homeschool year feels like swallowing an open fire hydrant in one gulp.

Before I began homeschooling, I imagined that my homeschool world would include three little girls in white dresses running in and out of the kitchen, the screen door slamming behind them as they tromped through the garden. I'd come outside with their nature journals, and we'd sketch and label and listen to the robins tweeting. Then we'd cuddle on our

11

white sofa with a read aloud to while away the afternoon. Maybe we'd read *The Secret Garden*, *Little Women*, or one of Jane Austen's offerings.

It didn't take long to discover little girls in white dresses get dirty, not every kid loves to nature journal, and some kids don't want to sit at all. Four kids on a sofa likely means territorial skirmishes, and white sofas in a family home are the epitome of unbridled homeschool optimism. Homeschooling has as many challenges as it has its charms.

With each family comes different challenges, but here are a few common ones:

Homeschool, in the beginning: the first homeschool year feels like swallowing an open fire hydrant in one gulp. Having all the kiddos in one place, trying to teach them something, anything, and making lunch, reading French sentences, and answering math questions — a multitasking expedition.

Peace and joy in the first year homeschool world feels like an unreachable goal. Sometimes the kids bicker more as relationships are being negotiated. Thinking time feels as endangered as a snow leopard on the beach. It's a challenge to find time alone that isn't on a toilet seat. And trying to keep up with housework? A mess is made right after one is cleaned. In what part of our day does actual homeschooling even happen?

In the beginning, a barrage of homeschool philosophies overwhelms as we soak ourselves in homeschool research, visit with established homeschool mamas, read homeschool blogs, and peruse homeschool books. This research provides ideas, but also provides proof that everyone else seems to know how to homeschool right, whereas the newbies swim in a sea of uncertainty, or drown, as it sometimes seems.

Slump month is a known thing in the homeschool community. Somewhere in February the fog and clouds settle in low, and solidly, at our river valley homestead nestled between mountains. Sometimes, the sun doesn't visit for weeks. After the excitement of the new year is long behind us, and the season of celebration ended, the only break to look forward to is spring, glorious spring.

> Homeschooling has as many challenges as it has its charms.

In my part of the world, there is a lot of snow in February, which we use for our entertainment and exercise, like snowman building, snowball fights, and cross-country skiing. There is also a lot of overcast; the clouds are hung so low I can't always see across the river, let alone past the edge of our lawn. These are the kind of days that make us want to do a workbook bonfire and watch movies all afternoon.

This is the time of year I sense the kids are ready to fly away from their routine like the geese at the neighbouring island in late fall. Extracurriculars become ordinary. Everyone wants to run through the meadows barefoot, climb every mountain, swim through the sea. A very *Sound of Music* feel.

A continual stream of irritations. The kids bicker about who gets to sit in the front seat. "Don't look at me like that." Another demands, "I want to sit in the front seat of the car this time." Someone else in the car bickers, "Move your feet out of the way." Someone doesn't want to share a footwell in the car with their sibling. Bickering and complaining can get on a mama's nerves. We're learning superhuman circus tricks as we try to maintain patience as we listen to yet another argument between siblings.

We fawn over them when they're tucked into bed, but if they're not in their pajamas when we've asked, if they took twenty minutes to find their toothbrush, or still have their light on after nine, our sweet bedtime wishes turn into lioness roars of exasperation.

Homeschool boredom is a reality: even when

we are in the early parts of our homeschool years, we mamas might feel bored. We're not chatting at the water cooler on breaks (what breaks?) and we aren't donning fashionable three-piece suits for our commute to the office. We chat with littler people much of the day and sometimes tire of hearing about Lego builds and Barbie houses.

Some days we might want to invite the postal person to sit for a cup of tea and listen to details of her delivery route instead. Teach enough kids the Preposition Poem, and you might find yourself questioning the meaning of life. Stare at that list of prepositions long enough and you might will, with laser-focused eyes, the *First Language Lessons* to blow into a thousand bits. (PS still it's a useful book!)

Homeschool is messy. Homeschooling isn't just happily watching our kids' interests and floating from one exciting activity to the next. When once we thought being at home all day meant we could maintain a tidier home, we discovered we live here: every room is used for something.

Some days we can't find erasers anywhere; until weeks later, we discover them growing under the sofa cushions like a nest of mice. Some days we've finally purchased all the ingredients for a science experiment, then discover the littlest brother dumped the entire bottle of citric acid into a box of baking soda. No experiment today!

The house entryway always needs sweeping, there will always be dishes by the sink, and you will never be asked to photograph for House & Home. No matter our cleanliness standards, everything will not stay clean at the same time.

Life gets in the way. You trip into an argument with your partner before you've served breakfast. Your mother gets sick, and you have to cancel everything to drive her to appointments, talk to medical personnel, and plan future care. Your neighbour calls to ask if you can care for their dog as they are away, because their dog is afraid of thunder and lightning. A friend needs to take their older child to a doctor's appointment in another city, and you're asked to look after their younger children for the day. There's no substitute teacher to call. Every day won't be on a homeschool train schedule.

> ...you mouth the words "help me" as the school bus drives by.

Homeschool burnout: if the notion of putting the kids on random buses doesn't sound like a joke anymore; if instead, you mouth the words "help me" as the school bus drives by, you might be experiencing homeschool burnout. If you find yourself reacting to kids' squabbles or perpetually irritated that a child won't show interest in his studies, by saying, "If you don't, then you're getting on that bus Monday morning," you might be experiencing homeschool burnout. If you have written "research the local school's telephone number" on your to-do list, and plan to learn the school registration process, or if you're spending more time lying on the couch and calling yourself an unschooler, homeschool burnout might be your diagnosis.

Homeschool burnout is not selective. Burnout doesn't come to moms who love homeschooling and moms who homeschool because everyone else is homeschooling. Burnout is not for classically focused homeschool mamas more than unschool mamas. Burnout isn't just for moms who work part-time or for a single parent homeschooling alone. Burnout doesn't arrive on your front step in the second year or the fifth. Burnout doesn't visit if you have five kids or just one, two, or nineteen (though I would guess burnout would happen faster with nineteen).

You love your kids. You came into this homeschool thing from the beginning before they were the size of a bean. Or you bounded into this homeschool thing when the kids were well into school because you discovered the brilliance and engaging nature of other homeschool kids. Or homeschooling just seemed like the best choice at the moment for many possible reasons.

You spend hours reading about learning, listening to podcasts, reviewing all sorts of books and curriculum. You buy games you think they'd love. You plan unit studies and field trips. You make sure they have a balance of healthy and fun foods. You consider the best extracurricular choices for their aptitudes and interests. You shower them with extras you can afford, but also challenge their entitlement tendencies. You love your kids.

Your homeschool benefits: the homeschool life isn't a perfect life, and certainly not an easy life, but it is a charmed life.

- ➢ You get to be with your kids.
- ➢ You get to know them deeply.
- ➢ You get to know the intricacies of your family unit.
- ➢ You get to facilitate their interests jointly.
- ➢ You get to watch their aptitudes unfold. You don't have to wake up early. Or you choose to.
- ➢ You don't have to drive away from your house in pajamas to drop off the kids at

school, or you can wear pajamas all day long.

➤ You don't have to don a dress-up wardrobe, or you can; yoga pants are just as effective.

➤ You don't have to buy low-quality food for easy lunches.

➤ You don't have to concern yourself about classmate bullying — you see bullying, and you're on it, because you birthed the bully too.

➤ You watch your kids choose when they want to hang out with their friends and how much time they want to invest in those friendships.

> The homeschool life isn't a perfect life, and certainly not an easy one. It is a charmed life.

➤ You don't have to fit random school events into your calendar.

➤ You don't have to pay for childcare, bus transportation, or indoor school shoes.

➤ You don't have to resist social trends, because your kids typically take longer to discover the trend exists.

➤ You don't have to facilitate afterhours homework unless you choose to.

- ➢ You don't feel compelled to dress your kids in fashion trends unless you want to.
- ➢ You get hugs at random times in the day.
- ➢ You get to read stories with them until they're teenagers because you can call that literary hour.
- ➢ You get to explore subjects like classical music, art history, world history, ancient history, economics, and political science for your elementary school-aged kids.
- ➢ You can teach home economics and make dinner at the same time or sew handmade masks for frontline healthcare workers.
- ➢ You can fit in errands whenever you want, and call errands a field trip.
- ➢ As the kids get older, you can fit in time to do what you like: read, write, build a home business, homestead, or pursue your version of creativity.

All these benefits are yours for the next twenty years or thereabouts. (The length of time depends on your number of kids, when you started, and if you homeschool through high school.) No matter the exact number, it's a whole lot of years. **Ultra-responsibility and endless effort required.**

With all these years of benefits, immense

responsibility is required. No pressure, but that sense of responsibility you have for your child's well-being and education stays with you no matter how many years you do this.

Homeschooling takes a lot out of mamas. It's a challenge to thrive, not just survive. Homeschooling is hard work, a challenge to plan and coordinate, an effort to continually observe our children, listen to their needs, facilitate their curiosities & aptitudes, and encourage them to engage others in healthy ways.

When putting that much effort into others, you'd better be taking care of yourself.
You've poured yourself into your children, providing them with every good thing: hot lunches, nature journaling, violin lessons, patience, and coloured gel pens. I hope you've determined how to take care of yourself as you are taking care of everyone else.

Take a good, hard, long look at yourself. How are you taking care of you?

May you enjoy all the charms of homeschooling. May you be encouraged and reminded you are amazing. May you remember you are as worthy and valuable as those for whom you care. May these words compel you to build into yourself self-care practices that help you thrive, not just survive.

Want to know why I homeschool? Because living in this vast world, discovering all the world has to offer is intriguing, fascinating, and energizes me. I wouldn't want to do life without my children, even for an abbreviated time. I want to learn about life with my family for the days we are given together.

How did I come to homeschooling?

I picked up a book on our spring vacation in a resort mountain town twelve years ago. I had a spare afternoon, and an opportunity to leave my three little girls with my husband and go out for a few hours, to soak up some quiet time doing whatever struck my fancy. A rare moment in that decade.

> My first thought: homeschooling is not an option for our family

There were no unfinished phone calls, no bookkeeping, no housekeeping, no childcare, no cares. I had a free afternoon, my husband wasn't on-call, and there weren't many of them as we had three kids under six.

I had finished my most recently borrowed library books. No other books were sitting on my nightstand. I was carefree and bookless.

I ventured to the chic bookstore on the main street, thumbed my way through the parenting section, and came upon a book by Lisa Rivero entitled: *The Homeschooling Option: How to Decide When It's Right for Your Family*.

My first thought: homeschooling is not an option for our family. I have way too much work already with three little girls. Because so many acquaintances were homeschooling, I thought I'd better find reasons why it wasn't right for my family.

I didn't see myself as someone looking for a mission to step outside the crowd, be different, not be mainstream.

I'm a mainstream kind of gal, I thought to myself.

I don't have kids with behavioural troubles in school, just a little sassiness, and argumentativeness at home. No one was complaining of bullying. If anything, my oldest was the social butterfly with bright ideas that kept her friends engaged in her grade two class. So, I continued to read that book to determine my arguments against homeschooling. Then I would be able to defend myself and get on with other things.

Was it the first chapter or the second, where I began to identify with the author's arguments?

Does public education inspire a desire for learning? Or do my children generally spend most of their time wrestling with their identity, responding to labels, and grappling with uncertain interactions with peers at school? Was this my experience in school too?

Did I learn what I needed to learn to become the unique person I was born to be by attending school?

Hmm. I had to admit that some of the arguments presented made a whole lot of sense and were consistent with my experience.

I still had questions. Isn't avoiding the school social issues just a way to attempt to create an unreachable utopia? Don't all the troubling interactions prepare children to grow up happier, more aware of who they are, and able to deal with conflict?

Wouldn't the lack of constant companionship with similarly aged peers make my children lonely? Does a lack of constant companionship with similarly aged peers make me feel alone as an adult? Not sure I have a friend the same age as me. Hmmm, do I even choose my friends based on age?

Nonetheless, who am I to decide their education? Isn't the government the most capable of determining what my children should learn, or what they should think is valuable? Wouldn't the school system prevent knowledge bits from being overlooked? I know I had educational gaps.

Though I am a regular and robust reader, and I have a post-secondary education, I'm not a trained teacher. I did not learn to teach a classroom. Even though I have taught my girls how to sound out letters, count numbers, explain why the sky is blue and why seeds grow into plants and why, if you drop that book from the top of a seventeen-foot high stairwell and it falls on someone's head, someone might die.

But above all, could I really live with my children all the time? No six-hour break to clean the house, no time to organize my world, and no time to zip off to the gym? If I'm around all the time, maybe they'd want a break from me!

So many thoughts were backstroking then front stroking in my head.

Maybe the way we did family life could change to accommodate my solitude and interests too. Hmm, perhaps I could start writing professionally.

As I read on, what enticed me most were the repeated testimonies of increasingly healthy relationships between family members. They appeared to enjoy spending life together. They chose to learn to live with their family and learn about the world together.

One week of reading, and I had a new vision

for my family life.

I imagined myself in a white flowing sundress, with three little girls in white flowing dresses, rushing about our quaint homestead on Prince Edward Island (because you can only homeschool where Anne of Green Gables lived, or maybe in Minnesota where Laura Ingalls lived). We would zip outside to enjoy the summer sunshine, weed the garden together, and enjoy afternoons reading together on our white sofa.

I wanted to enjoy my children for as long as we had each other. After one week of reading and re-reading this unforeseen selection, I surprised myself. We're going to step out of mainstream to learn about life and the world together.

Two years later, the three little girls had those flowing white dresses in their closets. We added a spritely little boy to our family. We moved to beautiful British Columbia instead of Prince Edward Island and began homeschooling. Fast forward to the present moment, a decade later: our choice to home educate was the right choice.

The only genuinely earth-quaking uncertainty...why did I buy a white sofa?

The girls have outgrown their penchant for frilly white dresses. Some days we spend more days learning how to relate to each other than we do about the world. My children continue to peel back the onion of who they are meant to be. We are, many days, not every day, happily learning to live and learn about life together.

And while I take care of them, I've been learning to take care of me.

WHY DO YOU HOMESCHOOL?

When you uncover and clarify your reasons, you will be able to look at what you need, what your children need, and work out a plan to take care of all of you.

What are the reasons that brought you to homeschooling? Why are you homeschooling still? The reasons that brought you might not be the same reasons that sustain you. Or maybe you have similar reasons now as when you first started, like my reason for freedom: yet, some days, the challenges still overwhelm. Some days it feels like perspective is like trying to see the forest through the trees or trying to see the charmed life through the challenges.

If you want to take care of you, be clear of the reasons you're doing what you're doing. When you uncover and clarify your reasons, you will be able to look at what you need, what your children need and work out a plan to take care of all of you.

Write down a list of the reasons you homeschool:

➢

➢

➢

➢

What makes homeschooling a joy for you?

➢

➢

➢

➢

What makes homeschooling a challenge for you?

➢

➢

➢

What self-care strategies do you regularly employ?

➢

➢

➢

➢

What self-care strategies do you need to strengthen?

➢

➢

➢

➢

What thoughts or feelings do you regularly grapple with?

➢

➢

➢

➢

➢

What was the reason you picked up this book?

➢

WHY SELF-CARE?

I don't think there's a profession out there that doesn't demand a need for self-care...if you're human, you need self-care.

Even before homeschooling, I was the kind of mama who tried to bounce a colicky baby on my knee while using the toilet (yes, I really did). I am the kind of mama who purchased, and read, heaps of popular parenting books instead of the more favourable equivalent of an all-inclusive vacation.

Self-care wasn't a widespread discussion when I began parenting eighteen years ago. Self-care wasn't part of the title of any book, and it certainly wasn't on my daily checklist. Self-care is something I had to learn. I am still learning.

Even before my four children arrived, I wasn't the kind of person that spent more than a minute walking through the drug store makeup aisle. I determined my lipstick colour in grade twelve. (Still going with that one — though I can only find it as Sephora's Rum Punch). I learned to apply makeup watching soap operas in the eighties. (I stopped watching soap operas, but I'm still going with those makeup techniques.)

> Self-care for my physical needs, my emotional needs and my mental needs weren't my instinct.

When I felt my efforts weren't good enough, I strove toward perfection, instead of accepting my aptitudes, efforts, and weaknesses. When I felt angry, I let my feelings rip (into whoever was nearest), blaming that person for my feeling instead of taking charge of that feeling. When I felt overwhelmed, I whipped myself into unreasonable expectations, and whipped those around me into a frenzy too. Self-care for my physical needs, my emotional needs, and my mental needs weren't my instinct.

I gradually came to understand I needed to take care of myself so I could continue homeschooling with a happy heart, or a mostly happy heart.

When my children were little, self-care meant I aspired to independently use the toilet, and occasionally showering. Now I have so many self-care strategies they could fill a book. (You may be holding it).

Early on, ignoring kids banging on the door was challenging. Auspicious days meant showering and prepping food for me, and countless baby latching hours sitting on the couch. Brushing my teeth was a gold star day. I had to save those 80s makeup techniques for the next decade.

Everyone needs self-care. Just yesterday, my husband, a physician, returned from a shift in emergency, waved hello to my friend and me, and said he was going to the other room to engage in a little self-care. That comment sounded funny coming from his mouth. I'm not sure I've ever heard him use that phrase, but after spending twelve hours assessing people's needs, trying to be a peaceful presence in many anxious moments, he needed to decompress.

My husband's version of self-care is a lot different than mine. He'll scan Twitter, exercise on the elliptical, lift weights, practice Chariots of Fire on the piano, run our dog up and down the hundred-foot driveway, chainsaw trees on our homestead, or play online chess. Not one of those things would be on my list.

I don't think there's a profession out there that doesn't demand a need for self-care. I don't claim to think self-care is more necessary for a homeschooling mama than a front-line emergency worker, an airline pilot, a line typist, or a restaurant hostess. Different stressors, different expectations, but if you're human, you need self-care.

Unique to the homeschooling mama is the continuous stream of her children's presence. There are moments of pure gratification: watching the kids harmoniously engage, pursuing new interests, jumping hurdles, and being the cute kids we brought into the world.

Do you know what's also ours? (I know you do.) A predictable, continuous stream of fledgling emotions, sibling bickering, complaining, distraction, and uncertainty in how to parent. I know you all have more to add to the list.

When my oldest was about eleven, I began to feel the creep of homeschool overwhelm. I was tired of the demands, and I was tired of my expectations, the way we were doing things. I was just tired. I didn't want to keep homeschooling if I felt miserable. I had to find a way to build boundaries, build into myself, and feed me too.

Self-care was a necessity, not an option.

I have homeschooled for ten years, through baby years, toddler years, adolescent years, and now the essay-checking University years. You don't have to tell me that you don't know how to fit everything in. I get you, girlfriend.

You're looking to take care of others, and you're not taking care of yourself? Some days you feel like Wonder Woman, understandably, but some days you collapse in bed with your teeth unbrushed, an ounce of chocolate and a Netflix app, and wake up bleary headed with your eye on the coffee machine.

> When we take care of ourselves, we can respond from a healthy place.

When you replenish you, you have something to give. When you're assuming this significant role, your kids need you to take care of you (then they'll know how to take care of themselves later too).

When you take care of yourself, you are living your life fully. When you take care of you, you can enjoy the homeschool job. (Let's clarify, you're not going to love your homeschool job all the time. That's not a thing.) But most of the time, would be ideal.

The most important reason to take care of

you is to healthfully engage your physical, mental and emotional practices so you can be purposeful in your homeschool mama role.

When I look back at the four significant homeschooling themes to which I have written, self-care is one of the largest. Self-care hasn't been my strong point. Instead, I have overcompensated for others' needs, made sure they were happy first, and if they weren't, I tried very hard to work toward their happiness. (Which, as you know, is unrealistic, and also, not the goal of parenting.)

Try as any parent might, we are easily consumed by our oft-repeated uncomfortable emotions. We have our heartstrings tied to our children's successes and failures, to their struggles and joys, to their disharmony and harmony.

When we take care of ourselves, we can respond from a healthy place. We then can distance our children's fledgling emotions from our egos, our sense of well-being, because quite simply, though they might have arrived through our womb, they are not us. Their choices are theirs. Their struggles are theirs. Their developmental stage is theirs. The unique stamp of personhood and their purpose in the world is theirs.

We are not the main character on their stage. We are the main character on our stage.

Our child is the main character on their stage.

However, we desire to hold their challenges though they are all ours. This is a constant temptation for the engaged parent. As homeschooling parents, we are most definitely engaged parents. So, we must take care to guard against hovering and helicoptering, co-depending or controlling, which don't benefit the kids anyway and takes way too much from ourselves.

The most powerful things I have learned as a homeschooling mama are to learn what I need, learn who I am and what makes me tick, what I'm interested in, what energizes me, and most definitely, what triggers uncomfortable feelings in me.

Triggers of all sorts. Repetitive loud noises when someone is asleep in the house, kids who complain when asked to help bring in groceries, kids not willing to get into the car when we need to get somewhere, or kids who don't want to practice violin even though they begged to play.

Self-care provides:

- ➢ consistent replenishing so we have something to give

> greater capacity to be present more of the time

> self-understanding of our triggers and learning to respond to them well

> perspective that our challenges are normal

> release from being responsible as homeschool mama all the time

Our goal is to experience an abundant homeschool life, the charmed life. We've got places to go, groceries to buy, percentages to explain, shirts to fold, and lessons to plan, so let's accept that self-care should be on our essential to-do list.

CARING FOR MAMA'S EMOTIONS

...our feelings continue as a perpetual river of unpleasant energy that infuses every aspect of our day and our relationships.

Homeschool mamas are human. We don't associate all those feelings with the homeschool experience. However, we are humans homeschooling, and it is human to be familiar with all these feelings.

We homeschool mamas accept satisfaction, contentment, glee, and delight as part of the homeschool experience. We expect these feelings.

Classic Homeschool Mama Struggles

Sadness. Boredom. Frustration. Irritation. Contentment. Disappointment. Rejection. Contempt. Satisfaction. Confusion. Annoyance. Delight. Ecstasy. Glee.

No homeschool mama thinks to herself: let me sign up for frustration, disappointment, aggravation, confusion, or impatience. We assume homeschooling will be fun, interesting, exciting, and at the very least, tolerable.

> …and I suspect I'll never let that fantasy go.

Homeschool utopia isn't anyone's reality, though it might have been our early homeschool mama expectation, whether we admit that or not.

Sometimes I find myself bored in our routine. Some days I am as enthused checking my kids' understanding of math concepts and helping them develop a piece of writing as they are enthused at putting the dishes away. Some days I wonder what it would be like to drop the kids off at school and spend my day writing about homeschooling. (Yes, I know what I just wrote).

Sometimes I find myself envying my husband as he influences the world outside our home. Some days I wonder what it would have been like to work as a nurse practitioner as I once thought I would. I experience these feelings despite having chosen my mothering and homeschooling path eagerly.

Some days I find myself irritated with sibling rivalry, bickering, and complaining. I wish I could intravenously infuse those days with energy, warmth, patience, and kindness. I feel irritated despite knowing kids don't grow up without rivalry, bickering, and complaining. I won't deny that this internal fantasy hasn't disappeared, and I suspect I'll never let that fantasy go.

Some days I feel frustrated enough to lose my temper, screech nonsensical words of complaint, then cry in the bathroom in shame and regret. Do I go for a long walk and abdicate all responsibilities? Do I apologize and call it a day with a bowl of popcorn and Curiosity Stream?

What to do with uncomfortable feelings? Journal them? Call a friend? Take a walk? Scream into a pillow? Let the floodgates open when my husband arrives home? Pray to ask these feelings to be removed from me?

Uncomfortable feelings are, well, uncomfortable. If you're like me and identifying emotions wasn't a thing in your childhood home, rather, feelings were a phenomenon we learned to pretend away, then we might not know how to identify our feelings.

If we don't acknowledge our uncomfortable feelings, like anxiety, anger, disappointment, boredom, or sadness, our feelings continue as a perpetual river of unpleasant energy that infuses every aspect of our day and our relationships.

Observe our feelings: what are we feeling? Do we know a variety of words to describe a variety of feeling states? Besides happy, mad, glad, or sad?

Acknowledge our feelings: life transformation begins the moment we allow ourselves to experience our feelings in all their occasional glory or occasional unpleasantness. We learn about ourselves, others, and life when we acknowledge our feelings.

Instead of judging our feelings as good or bad, instead of guilting or shaming ourselves for having a feeling, we can just observe the feeling and get familiar with it. We learn why we feel what we do.

Why does it get under our skin that our kiddo can't grasp a math concept? Sometimes we must learn about learning and how individuals process new concepts. Sometimes our expectations are unrealistic. We assume the worst and futurize, "She'll never learn." Or we want

Teresa L. Wiedrick

to make sure that when Grandma asks about a math concept, our child sounds like she's at the level of her same-aged peers.

How often we discover some unresolved hurt arising from a feeling we have been denying. When we accept our feelings wherever we're at. (No matter how absurd they might sound if we put words to them). When we say hello to them, and make friends with them, their intensity gradually lessens. Cheesy, but accurate.

> Awareness and wisdom arise with honest acknowledgement about our internal world

Unlike any other self-care tip, this self-care practice can profoundly influence our satisfaction. The instant we begin observing ourselves, allowing our feelings to exist, and accepting them as they are, we are able to unlock intense or confused feelings. Awareness and wisdom arise with honest acknowledgement about our internal world.

Sometimes we accept our

uncomfortable feelings and sometimes we reframe our uncomfortable feelings. Attending a seminar with Dr. Daniel Amen, author of *Change Your Brain, Change Your Life*, was my first introduction to these three compelling questions:

> ➤ Is what you think true?

> ➤ Are you sure your thought is true?

> ➤ If there was another perspective, what might be the natural outcome of that new perspective?

I add to these questions:

> ➤ Brainstorm five possible outcomes to your thought because our thoughts influence the outcome.

> ➤ Then choose the best possible thought, the one that will work most favourably for your desired outcome.

If you have chosen to homeschool, if you have decided homeschooling is worth your energy and time, then commit to addressing uncomfortable feelings when they arise. Own them, question them, get curious, and reframe them so you can be present in your homeschool the way you want to be.

Classic homeschool mama struggles are akin to the human struggle. Accept your uncomfortable feelings in all their messy, unpleasant manifestations. You've got this girlfriend.

SELF-DIFFERENTIATION: YOU BECOMING YOU

If you're always trying to be normal, you will never know how amazing you can be.
-Maya Angelou

How YOU are you? Self-differentiation is the intention to be oneself while living alongside others. It seems evident on the exterior that we are separate from our family members. In practice, though, self-differentiation is less obvious. We are separate from our children. Hard as this might seem in the all-consuming, early homeschool days, we even have an identity outside the realm of a homeschool mom.

Who are you apart from your partner and children? Are you fully versed in your identity separate from them? Do you engage in activities that are distinctly you? There comes a time when we recognize that though we passionately appreciate and enjoy the homeschool mom role, we are also a person outside that role.

You were a person apart from them before they existed. What did you do when you had spare time on a weekend afternoon? Were you out late on a Saturday or were you a Sunday afternoon brunch goer?

I was neither. As a struggling college student, I preferred cheap movies on Friday night, an occasional breakfast at Denny's on Saturday mornings, and wandering through Chapters with Starbucks in hand any Sunday afternoon. Otherwise, I worked as a night shift labour and delivery unit clerk and studied for my nursing science degree.

> ...we even have an identity outside the realm of a homeschool mom.

To this day, these are things I love (minus the nursing night shifts). I still love reading, writing, watching films, and gardening. I rarely eat at a Denny's; compliments to the hens at my

50

Cluckingham Palace (sixty feet outside my front door).

Learning to maintain our sense of self while maintaining a relationship is a challenge. As a mama of young kids, there is a thin line between us and our children. If young kids need us, we respond immediately. When we function as a homeschool mama long enough, small kids turn into big kids. Because those big kids stay with us for years, and they need us no matter their age, we are accustomed to responding to them with the same presence no matter their age.

We're the nurturers, the teachers, and the uber mamas. We live right beside our children in the next room or down the hall. Our children's emotional needs, interpersonal needs, educational needs, physical needs, transportation needs, and financial needs are ever-present. Seeing ourselves as separate from our role as our children's mother as we attend to their accomplishments, struggles, and needs, can be a challenge.

Self-differentiating allows us to own our different opinions, interests, and values despite our family member's differing opinions, interests, or values. It also means we're learning to maintain an emotional connection with our family members *despite* those differences.

Why all this discussion on self-differentiation? Because it doesn't take long into our homeschool life to forget we have an identity outside our children. Our goal is to maintain a connection with our children while also maintaining a separate sense of self. This is especially challenging when we are with our children most of the time.

Has this happened to you? A child stands in front of you, frustrated, afraid, or anxious, and you don't understand why she feels what she's feeling. You know your feelings aren't hers and you wouldn't respond the way she's responding to this specific scenario. Her uncomfortable feelings trigger different feelings in you, perhaps frustration or confusion. What are you going to do with your feelings?

The more we know ourselves, the greater clarity we have about others too. When we understand ourselves, we more easily recognize the impact we have on others and how others impact us. We more easily accept others' complicated feelings when we can accept our own.

How to Practice Self-Differentiation in our Families:

> **Observe family interactions.** Learn how we affect our children. If we're having a

bad day, do we infuse our children's days with unpleasant energy? (I know I can). How do our children affect us? Do they, at times, infuse our day with unpleasant energy? (Trick question.)

➢ **Understand others' feelings.** Others' feelings, no matter how woo woo they seem to us in a moment, need to be acknowledged and respected. Even when...you fill in the blank.

➢ **Collect the kids.** Start the day gathering the kids with a warm hug or a sunny "Good morning" before you do anything else. This infuses warm energy, which affects how they engage each other too. It's also a great assessment tool. When a kiddo doesn't want a hug, it speaks volumes about where they're at and how they might influence their siblings. One grouchy child at breakfast will likely affect the rest of the kids. Two cranky kids make for a heck of a drive to town. Three grouchy kids might be a pseudo-nuclear meltdown. But just one persistently irritable kid will exhaust us by dinnertime even still.

➢ **Explore your messy family dynamics to**

determine how the interplay bears out. How does the state of your marriage affect your children? How does sibling rivalry affect you, and how do you affect your children's sibling rivalry? How does your partner influence each child? How does each of your children affect others? How do these interactions affect random strangers, extended family members, or community members? How does all this affect your well-being? (Is this paragraph so messy, you'd rather me just delete it?)

-Who are you in challenging family dynamics? The ability to be emotionally separate, to not become mired with another's emotions, is the challenge. It is a challenge to maintain peace in demanding scenarios and continue enjoying the homeschool family life despite the mess.

-Enmeshment is easy in family relationships. We're with each other often and when others are content and happy, it makes our lives easier. It is easy to give advice when it's not requested. It's easy to be reactive when we feel offended. It is easy to worry instead of strategically planning. It is easy to feel threatened by kids' contrariness. It is easy to withdraw from family members, instead of acknowledging our feelings and asking for our needs to be met. It is too easy to blame others instead of taking responsibility for our feelings. It is easy to become compliant or play the peacekeeper and not acknowledge our needs. It is easy to make assumptions (or mind-read) and not ask our family members what they feel or what they need. It is too easy to be overly serious or joke inappropriately at someone's expressed needs.

> ...they have their emotional mountains to climb too.

➢ Learn to take care of yourself, to self-soothe, when you feel intense emotions. Self-soothing is a lifetime practice of becoming aware of our thoughts and emotions and learning how to engage them. Allow yourself to feel the feelings. Breathe through uncomfortable feelings. Counsel yourself in front of a mirror. Tap your legs back and forth. Take a walk. Lie on a yoga mat.

➢ Accept that no one wants to make you feel frustrated; they have their emotional mountains to climb too. Not even the grouchy teenage girl. Nope. Not even her. Our children might engage in immature ways at times, but their intent isn't to frustrate us.

➤ **Give up your family-perfect delusions.** Do you have expectations of perfection from your family-of-origin? Do you believe you can create a perfect family? Perfect isn't a thing.

The goal is to be emotionally independent: to recognize our feelings and be able to share them when appropriate, to request what we need, and to honour those requests from those around us.

> **"If you're always trying to be normal,**
> **you will never know how amazing you can be."**
> **Maya Angelou**

TAKING CARE OF BOUNDARIES

Boundaries are simply this: you respect yourself and expect others to respect you also.

We homeschool mamas have a unique challenge and privilege all at the same time: we signed up to be with our children. We might need a little quiet in our homes. We might need some time away from our kids. We might need a clean house in order to feel sane. That's a challenge.

Boundaries are simply this: you respect yourself and expect others to respect you also.

Why build boundaries? The boundaries you maintain around your energy, needs, and goals will help you maintain your peace, quiet, cleanliness and organization. When our needs and goals are met, we have energy and mental space to extend nurture to those around us too.

What kinds of boundaries do we instill? Boundaries are entirely subjective. What you value and what I value aren't the same. Maybe you don't value a clean house. I've met that mom. She was horribly messy, but also far more content with her kids. To each her own.

We need to create at-home work boundaries. Some of us moms are trying to work from home while homeschooling. For my creative writing to expand, I like to write in quiet. *Mwahaha.* (You know where I'm going). This has been a challenge, to say the least. Over the years my kids have learned (most days) if I am tapping on my laptop or my study door is closed, I am unavailable.

> ...you do not have to be a representative of the homeschool world.

We need to create morning boundaries. I insist on fifteen minutes of early morning quiet for my brain to wake up with a cup of coffee, daily reading, and a journal entry. As I'm aging, I wake at ridiculously early hours, so I don't have to work at it. Teenagers don't wake at 5.

How to accomplish morning boundaries with younger kids: For some three-year-olds, fifteen minute's quiet might be too long. Consider purchasing an alarm clock and set the alarm to 7 o'clock. They're up at six, you say. The alarm clock is for them to stay IN their room. Let them know when the alarm goes off, they can come out and greet you then. Make sure they're set up with a few toys, books, and a snack just for the morning, so they have something to do. (And I know, this idea would never have worked with one of my girls, but it worked with the other three.)

Build on your time apart. Consider setting a boundary on your toilet time. If the door is closed, no one can talk to you, unless the house is on fire. Direct them to scream, THE HOUSE IS ON FIRE! And the house better be on fire. Stretch toilet time to ten minutes, then eleven, then twelve. Bring in a book and a cup of coffee. (At what age do you start? If they don't know what a fire is, or they don't have the verbal skills to yell, "The house is on fire," they're too young.)

Build boundaries with non-supporters. When you're not feeling the love from the general public or an unsupportive relative, when you regularly hear comments like "Why aren't you in school? Is it legal? Do you have teaching certification?" Remind yourself: you do not have to be a representative of the homeschool world. People are often just surprised by an unconventional choice or wondering if there's a holiday. They might benefit from hearing your reasons for your homeschool preference. If you've been asked something regularly, be prepared to answer, but determine your answers in advance. No sass required.

Build boundaries into your homeschool day. If you're not an unschooler, and you're occupied in a study routine, don't answer the phone. Determine your study hours, let the regular people in your life know those study hours, and they will learn to honour them as you insist these boundaries are as necessary as punching a clock in a workplace.

Build cleanliness boundaries. Maybe you want to teach your kids, "Keep your room clean, flush the toilet after you use it, wash your hands after you use the toilet, wipe the bathroom wall after you pee (boy mamas unite!)." You can teach them whatever is essential to you. Yes, the wall will still gradually yellow because they are learning. They're not mini janitors. But you gotta start somewhere.

Teach kindness boundaries. Teach them not to interrupt their siblings. Be patient. However, assume their immaturity in relating continues throughout childhood. Teach them to listen to each other and to you. Teach them to repeat back what they've heard their sibling say so they actually learn how to listen. Expect great things from their sibling relationships and assume this is the ultimate training ground for future relationships.

Caveat: small children are natural boundary breakers. If you have small children, the notion of boundaries is nebulous at best. What boundaries do you expect from a child who is six? Or ten? How about fifteen? Just remember, kids don't get magic boundary pills. You gotta teach 'em.

Assume boundaries will take a while to learn. Assume you really will be repeating yourself a million times. Give yourself a break: expect boundaries won't be established quickly or without mistakes. *Boundaries are taught over time.*

Teresa L. Wiedrick

TAKING CARE OF MAMA'S THOUGHTS

Sign up for parenting, sign up for doubts.

We also need to take care of the boundaries in our minds. How many thoughts do we think in a day? Lots going on up there. Ever sit for a few minutes and try not to think at all?

Hold your middle fingers to your thumbs, then rest them on your crossed legs on a yoga mat in a quiet place in the house. (Okay, I lost you when I suggested there was a quiet place in your home.)

If you've sat to meditate for any moment ever, or attempted to quietly listen to God, without listening to your own anxious, organizing, or preoccupied thoughts, you've discovered your thoughts move faster than clouds in a stormy sky.

The more you sit to listen (also known as meditation), the more you observe your thoughts, the more you recognize you are not your thoughts. You are separate from them. Why would we sit to listen to them? Don't we have enough thoughts in the day? We have stuff to do.

> ...sometimes, when we ascribe the incorrect meaning to those feelings, we get ourselves into trouble.

Many of those thoughts aren't helpful, aren't equivocally true, and sometimes create more trouble when we respond to them as though they were true.

Have you considered that your thoughts are separate from you? (No, I'm not suggesting you hear voices.) We have many, many thoughts. If we sit long enough, in a quiet place (where there aren't little voices or to-do lists screaming), we discover there is a still person behind the thoughts: a person behind the worried, frustrated, uncertain, sad, or concerned thoughts.

Though our thoughts have a reason to exist, it's also true that some thoughts aren't helpful. On a particular day, I might think: the kids will grow up to live in an dilapidated cabin they found up an abandoned mining road because the bank won't risk lending them money, no one will befriend them, and no one will employ them. The signs are there: they grab their siblings' toys too often, demand they get whatever toy they want, they don't finish their work, and they spend every nickel given to them.

Feelings and thoughts are part of the human experience. We feel our feelings. We think our thoughts. Much of the meaning we ascribe to those thoughts or feelings isn't always accurate. And sometimes, when we ascribe the incorrect meaning to those feelings, we get ourselves in trouble.

Like the anxious thoughts that worry that we're not going to get everything done in a day. What exactly will happen if we don't get our to-do list completed? Will the house explode? Will the children wilt into the compost pile? Will the social worker remove the children from our home because we didn't return the dentist's reminder call to get their teeth checked?

Or like the angry thoughts that say, "She shouldn't have said that to me. I have to make her understand, or she will not maintain a relationship past "hello" when she grows up."

What would happen if we told ourselves a different story about those thoughts? What if we told ourselves we might have put too many things on our to-do list? Or that our child will eventually learn how to speak respectfully because they are watching their respectful parents be kind.

Do you notice how some days those thoughts come out rather negatively? "Oh no," we think to ourselves as we see someone we didn't want to see, "not that person again." Or, "There she goes again, getting upset with her sister." Or, "The flab on my tummy is not going away," as I munch on another potato chip.

> Instead of allowing the fuel of unhelpful thoughts barrage our already busy lives, we need to practice responding to them.

Do you notice how some days those thoughts come out rather positively? You hear the kids squabble and think, "They'll figure it out. Just a learning opportunity in relationships." You answer the phone even though you don't recognize the phone number and hope you can be a warm spot to an underpaid telemarketer's day. Or you think, "I like how my non-photoshopped, non-regularly-exercised body reveals a lifetime of stories."

Our thoughts are fleeting. Some days we have better perspective than other days. This is the human experience.

Ever hear of positive thinking challenges? "Don't think anything negatively for a week; it'll change your life." I know I couldn't do it so I would just be disappointed in myself. (How negative of me, ha.) Instead, I'll slowly plod through my thought-life one day at a time, focus on one thought at a time, and try to explore what's going on in my brain and reframe as I go. *Positive thinking challenges begone!*

However, analyzing my thought life, acknowledging that this is who I am, I feel frustrated when … I feel sad when … I feel overwhelmed when … I feel shamed when … leads to understanding ourselves which facilitates a quieter internal state.

So, when I have challenging feelings, I can ask myself once again:

1. What is the thought behind the feeling?
2. Is the feeling true?
3. Am I one hundred percent certain the feeling is true?
4. If the feeling isn't true, perhaps there can be a natural conclusion that doesn't have such a dramatically imagined consequence.

What are we going to do about our thoughts,

both pleasant and unpleasant ones?

Instead of allowing the fuel of unhelpful thoughts barrage our already busy lives, we need to practice responding to them.

It doesn't serve us to pretend they don't exist, though many people are very good at telling themselves they can. We can ignore that someone really hurt us and pretend the hurt away for the sake of harmony. We can pretend that when our child ignores our request, we don't feel angry. When we're honest with our feeling thoughts, we have a chance to address them. Otherwise, how do we address something we can't identify?

When we learn to acknowledge what needs to be changed, we can let go of what we can't change.

> ➤ Yep, I feel uncertain for my child's future when my child asks if she can try public school.
> ➤ Yep, I feel afraid when my daughter wants to get her driver's license.
> ➤ Yep, I feel angry when my child sasses me in front of her Grandma.

If you're like me and grew up with no discussion on feelings, no discussion on your inner world, you might find it challenging to identify your feelings. *We need to spend time getting comfortable with our thoughts.* We can't deal with emotions we don't know we have, so *give them space.*

Feelings are more difficult to differentiate if you don't acknowledge them when they're happening. It can be like the metaphorical dog hair clinging to a piece of fleece. One feeling upon another feeling, layers, and layers of uncomfortable feelings, woven together like a mohair sweater.

Some of our thoughts need paper and pen: writing them down helps to clarify what we think, and often disarms their intensity. As part of our homeschool writing, I have always included journaling with my kids' daily studies. Learning to identify our feelings is step number one. Whether our kids write, "I hate my life," or "I hate mom," or "I hate my sister," or whatever unpleasantries they may record, it is a useful starting point to learn to identify feelings. We can do that too.

Check your thoughts periodically by writing in a morning journal. Identify the unpleasant feelings; relish the pleasant ones. You don't have to do anything with the record of your feelings. Just ponder and acknowledge them.

Journal your memories, dreams, and interpersonal interactions. Vent your frustrations without hurting anyone's feelings.

Some of our thoughts need an ear. Maybe a friend, spouse, or someone objective, like a counselor. Some friends are not useful in hearing our thoughts, either because they don't have answers, they have too many answers, or they encourage blame and don't encourage taking responsibility. Sometimes we choose to talk to friends because we don't want to work on the struggle. We want to blame and get sympathy instead of doing something. Choose your listening ears wisely.

Some of our thoughts need quiet space. Meditation, which is just listening to our thoughts, is effective. Sitting, quietly, breathing slowly, allowing our thoughts to diffuse, often helps us gain clarity about what's inside.

We need to address our thoughts like a well-argued lawyer. I'll reiterate because it bears practicing over and over: Is what we feel true? Is it possible our thoughts aren't accurate? Is it possible we could have a different perspective if we thought something different? And this different perspective might influence us toward taking different actions?

Some of our thoughts might require us to

change our behaviour because our behaviour makes us feel something we don't want to feel.

We can't tackle all our feelings at once. However, we can try these thought experiments from Psychology Today author Hal Shorey, Ph.D., Professor of Clinical Psychology at Widener University's Institute of Graduate Clinical Psychology:

1. Look up from your screen and observe your surroundings. Suspend judgment and think about this thought independent of your feelings. Is there anything wrong in this moment? Many who do this exercise will respond "No." Sometimes we focus too much on what has happened in the past or on our painful stories. Really, though, everything is okay right now.

2. If you lost your memory tonight and could not recall any painful past, would your day be different tomorrow? Would you go about your day and enjoy the things you see and the people you encounter?

3. Daydream. Imagine you are in a different world. How might you carry yourself or see yourself in the world? Would you feel differently? Allow the emotions and thoughts of that other form to come into your body.

4. Look into your eyes in the mirror and ask, "What am I?"

If you're going to make up a story, make sure the story serves you. We need to acknowledge our thoughts, recognize when they're limiting us, recognize how some of our thoughts create limitations in our lives, and determine to take actions that help us create a story that serves us.

Let's chat about some of the thoughts we grapple with as homeschool mamas.

"We don't sit in meditation to become good meditators. We sit in meditation, so we'll become more awake in our lives." Pema Chodron

Grappling with Doubt

Doubt: that five-letter word that occasionally occupies parents who choose a less than conventional educational approach for their children.

You don't have to be a homeschool parent to have parenting doubts. Have a child? Have doubts. Am I giving him what he needs? Am I influencing him in the right direction? When she acts unpleasantly, is her action a reflection of how I'm engaging her? Is she getting enough of an academic challenge? Am I helping him connect with others effectively?

Sign up for parenting, sign up for doubts.

When you hold that little one in your hands for the first time, you also hold a world of uncertain potentials. Will the baby survive the night in her crib? The first time she eats solids, will she choke? Should I immunize, or will I induce harm? Should I leave her to cry it out or baby carry?

Doubt exists in every choice we make as parents. Doubt comes with the territory. We feel the serious responsibility of imprinting a human, teaching her what she needs to know about morality, about people, about purpose, and about feelings. We want to encourage her to follow her interests and develop her aptitudes. All this and we're also trying to keep her alive through the toddler and teenage years.

Accept the human experience: there is no way not to doubt your choices. We experience the feeling of uncertainty in all sorts of realms. *Parenting perfection isn't a thing, no matter what choices we make.* We weren't designed to play God for our children. We were intended to lead, guide, and direct, love, nurture, and provide for them. Perfect parenting isn't a possibility — it would be as possible as countering gravity in our earthly existence.

Do what you can with what you know. Then Maya Angelou reminds us, *"When you know to do better, do better."*

Parenting is a process that enables us to take a close look at ourselves. Our children are one of our mirrors that help us see ourselves more clearly. Just as we were placed in our children's lives, our children were placed in our lives. We're teaching each other. What we see will not always be pleasant, but when we set ourselves on a path of growth, we will grow.

> Usually, there is a doubt behind the doubt.

Choose the less conventional homeschool lifestyle and it is guaranteed that you will hear others express their doubts.

The homeschool lifestyle introduces a whole new series of doubts. Uncertainty is a regular discussion point when chatting with new homeschool mamas. Often new homeschool mamas want to be shown the ropes so their anxieties can be quelled so they can be assured they're doing it right.

Not following the culture naturally makes people question themselves. Having a constant stream of questions about socialization and academics feeds our uncertainties. There's a continuous dribble of outsider worries manifesting in "helpful questions," like "What if your child misses something? What if your child wants to go back to school? Are the child's aptitudes comparable to other similar-aged kids?" There is always a "helpful question."

Be surrounded by 99.7 out of 100 families of schoolchildren who are doing something different than us (those are the stats for registered homeschooling families in the province where we lived in 2012), and even the most fearless would surely doubt themselves at some point.

No matter our academic expectations, we still feel doubt. I know a homeschool mama who expresses uncertainty in her child's educational path, despite her child's faithful attendance in high school online classes, despite her daughter gobbling up university-level books on Renaissance art, despite her eagerness to memorize the Periodic Table of Elements, despite her professional violin training and competition wins — and yet, the child is only twelve. Still, her mom worries she isn't providing an adequate education.

The rest of us regular folk, with kids who prefer playing on screens and snapping photos for Snapchat, have parental doubts too. We bring out the Latin book and dabble in Duolingo or Rosetta Stone. We teach grammar, dictation, and spelling. We practice mental math questions on road trips and expect research papers on comparative governments. Yet we still wonder if what we're doing is what "they're doing" down the street, at the brick and mortar school.

Unschooling parents have doubts. Classical Homeschooling parents have doubts. Charlotte Mason-based parents have doubts. Everyone has doubts.

We first need to put words to our doubts. What is the reason behind a doubt? Usually, there is a doubt behind the doubt.

Doubt arises in all sorts of homeschool forms:

> ➢ I don't think I'll be able to teach my child to read.

> ➢ I'm not sure my math skills are strong enough to teach my children.

> ➢ My kiddo is introverted: should she be in a class of twenty-five to expand her horizons?

> ➢ I don't feel organized on the best of days. How do I organize a child's education?

➢ Can I really trust unschooling to serve my child's academic needs?

➢ The local public school is providing an aquarium or robotics program — obviously, I can't. Maybe my children would be better served at a school.

➢ Should I choose the curriculum I overbought last year or the one everyone else has recently purchased?

➢ Should I choose the Charlotte Mason or Susan Wise Bauer's philosophy of homeschooling?

➢ What if my child doesn't meet academic peer levels?

➢ Oh no! I see gaps in my kids' education.

➢ My kiddo says he hates homeschooling!

So many doubts, so little time.

Some of our doubts can be silenced simply by acknowledging them. Say them out loud. Some need a little more effort.

If we've grappled with this doubt before, we've reasoned it through, and we've determined how we will act, then we must render that feeling again and again.

Deep breathe. Take a deep breath and allow that feeling to pass, again. Sometimes there is nothing we can do to make the uncertainty go away. We need to accept "not knowing" as part of the human experience. Doubt is undoubtedly part of the parenting experience. We cannot predetermine everything.

Some doubts are addressed head-on. Write your doubts on a piece of paper. Brainstorm every possible thing that could go wrong. Research possibilities that could counter the validity of those doubts. Determine to worry on paper. Once a day. Then determine what the best approach for that struggle is today. Do that again tomorrow morning if the struggle is acute. Or if it isn't acute, schedule that doubt for next Tuesday morning at 6 am sharp. If you can worry about it later, worry about it next week.

> Sometimes the reasons we start homeschooling aren't the reasons we continue.

Act on your answer; question your doubts. Ask yourself why you first chose to homeschool. What compelled that decision? What were you hoping you would gain from homeschooling? Answer those questions and regularly remind yourself of the answers.

Refine your answers. Sometimes the reasons we start homeschooling aren't the reasons we continue. We may have tripped into homeschooling because we recognized something our children needed that school couldn't provide. In the first weeks of homeschool, we may have watched a transformation in our child's joy and ease. Perhaps we saw our overall family harmony increase. When we've been homeschooling for a while, we identify the engaging education even we parents gain. We recognize the increased time we gain, both in our schedule and in our children's schedule. We see that our children are more confident and secure. We create sweet memories that we didn't have when they were in school. Determine the reasons you are still homeschooling.

Recognize when you begin doubting yourself because others doubt you. If it weren't enough that we doubt ourselves, we also assume the doubts of those around us. It's too easy to fall into that trap in many areas of life. If we judge ourselves through the eyes of judgmental others, we will always find ourselves wanting. Most people don't care about our choices as much as we might think. We need to practice setting mental boundaries with other people's opinions.

Meditate or pray. Be still and listen to the small voice. Speak to the One who made you, speak to the One who planted this homeschool purpose inside you, and listen to the One who is leading you still. This step right here will cement certainty beyond anything else.

> Remember, it is these smiles, these faces, and these young people whom you wanted to homeschool.

Get on with what you're doing. You will continuously fine-tune what you're doing the longer you do it. You'll also refine why you're doing it.

Try to focus on enjoying the process. For all the efforts you put into your family life, practice enjoying the process. Enjoy watching the moments of connection between your children when they occur. Absorb the moments of book discussions and their newest artistic creations. Enjoy watching them explore new areas of life and relish in your homeschool world. Or, on the days when it seems too challenging to relish anything, at least practice enjoying it.

Remember, it is these smiles, these faces, and these young people whom you wanted to homeschool. *Enjoy your journey, enjoy your choices, and enjoy your kiddos.*

Grappling with Anger

I'm like every other mama. I don't like it when my kids complain, sass, irritate each other, argue over inane stuff, waste time, dawdle, and I don't enjoy listening to whining. I have my triggers. You have yours. While we may decrease our reactions to those triggers as life goes on, we do all have triggers and feel angry at times. It's called being human.

I don't like seeing myself angry, and anger in others provokes fear in me. I don't like seeing anger in me, because I don't want to shame or disrespect another person. If I am the angry one, am I showing others I don't like them? Yet, still, I'm human and I get irritated.

Everyone has their triggers. Sometimes after I feel angry, I determine I didn't have a good reason. Like getting upset when someone accidentally breaks something. Like expressing my annoyance when I am premenstrual. You may not identify with the reasons I shared, and you might add different reasons.

Expecting not to get angry is unrealistic.

Should we feel angry with our children? Why do we think we should never feel angry with our children? Can we all be honest? We're human. Anger is a human experience.

Sometimes the reason for our anger is because we attempt to control our children. That child may have grown in our womb and then we pushed her into the world. That child may have grown for the first eighteen years or more in our home, but that child was always a separate individual, separate from our partner and us. They were meant to be born into our families, meant to learn from us, and intended for us to learn from them. They are not calculations, products, or formulas as much as most parenting books would suggest. They are unique humans.

> They are not calculations, products or formulas as much as most parenting books would suggest.

Children need our direction. Our mentorship cannot be controlled. Some of their behaviour is childlike. We feel angry when one child bashes their brother because he won't return a Lego piece. We feel angry when we try to do something good for them, like get them to soccer practice on time, yet they complain and stomp their feet when they're asked to find their shin pads and socks. We feel angry when everyone has been asked to be quiet for their shift-worker dad, yet the moment dad's head hits the pillow, someone slams a door or yells to her sister to meet him on the trampoline. Childish behaviour, because they're children.

Feeling angry means you're normal. Of course, you feel angry. Anger is an uncomfortable emotion that takes the wind out of our sails, can trigger a boatload of trouble and resentment, but it's also a healthy reaction to many scenarios. Anger can dissolve a day into tears. *Anger feels uncomfortable for a reason.*

I wish I had known this earlier in my parenting: the angry feeling will pass. Anger is just a feeling. Feelings pass quicker sometimes than clouds in the sky.

> Feelings pass quicker sometimes than clouds in the sky.

We don't want to live in a state of anger with our kids. We mostly like them, most days. Some more than others on some days. (Okay, seriously, don't look at me like that. You know it's true.)

What to do about anger?

> ➤ **Get curious about your anger.** I have many unproud stories of when I did not engage anger in the right way. Sometimes I've been quick to assume the

worst and overreact. Determine to get curious. Why does someone's reaction trigger a feeling in me?

➢ **Observe yourself**. Lay on a yoga mat or your bed, wait till the heat passes, ask for understanding, and listen to yourself.

➢ **Go away**. Specifically, somewhere where your kids are not. Sometimes you are just in a state of overwhelm and it takes less stimuli to irritate you.

➢ **Accept that angry outbursts will interrupt your homeschool days**. These kids are learning to manage their emotions as we are still, too (they have less experience). Anger happens spontaneously and usually interrupts important stuff. Yes, even in the middle of a lesson. Expect angry, annoying interruptions to occur in the middle of homeschool days.

➢ **Breathe, breathe, breathe.** Breathe deeply and breathe slowly.

➢ **Write down your thoughts.** Writing facilitates understanding yourself. What got you exasperated? Okay, now that you have written that it annoyed you to watch your kid drawing in the corner of her math book instead of doing the math, ask yourself, "Why did you feel angry?" Write your answer, such as: "She doesn't care about the lesson I planned. Does she never do what I ask?" In a cooler moment, you can consider why you need her to care about those lessons.

➢ **Recognize underlying concerns**. What's underneath those thoughts? Do you need to know she'll get the math concept and not grow up unable to apply to a university program? Are you afraid you're incapable of teaching her? Are you rushed to do another activity and don't want to invest in this one? Consider your underlying concerns.

➢ **Sometimes doing nothing is the best option when you're feeling angry**. You can take a break from most of the kids' behaviours until a time when you're no longer in a triggered place. Then you can determine what you will do. Most scenarios don't worsen by doing nothing.

➢ **Determine how you want to engage your child.** Do you want them to cool down so they can try again to speak respectfully? Do you want them to have another chore in place of the one they were asked to do but didn't do? Do they need a hug and need to be heard? The goal: plan before you act.

➤ **Expect you won't hit the sweet spot every time**. If anger is a challenge for you like it has been for me, remind yourself that you're learning right alongside your children. Be as gracious with yourself as you are with them.

Remember you're teaching your children how to deal with anger by modeling how to engage your own anger. **These affirmations can be helpful (and also how you teach your children):**

➤ I will stay calm in frustrating situations.

➤ I must learn to manage my anger.

➤ Controlling my anger is natural to me.

➤ I always speak my mind, rather than let frustrations build.

➤ I control my anger by expressing myself in a firm yet positive manner.

➢ I am in control of myself.

➢ Being calm, relaxed, and in control is normal for me.

➢ I have the power to regulate my emotions.

➢ Managing anger will help to repair and strengthen my bonds with my friends and family.

➢ I owe it to myself to manage my anger.

➢ I can channel my anger in a more productive way.

➢ I am calm, focused, and relaxed.

Most importantly, be gracious with yourself as you learn to grapple with your anger and theirs.

"The best answer to your anger is silence."

Marcus Aurelius

Grappling with Failure

> "I get up. I walk. I fall down.
> Meanwhile, I keep dancing."
> Daniel Hillel

We all have those days when it doesn't matter what I do to admonish that child to be kind. When one of the kids wants to challenge everything that I say. When one of the kids wants to report everything that her sibling is doing wrong. When a child declares she can no longer read, compute basic arithmetic calculations, or spell three-letter words,

> Those days make me feel like a failure, not good enough.

though she's been doing those things for years. (And I say a few not-so-choice words about laziness.)

Those days, the ones when I wake up a little heavy, the world seems bright outside my bedroom window, but not inside my head. My head feels like the middle of February with its overcast and dreary skies. I have a solid dose of premenstrual tension. By the time I reach the kitchen, the kids are speaking thirty decibels louder than my head can manage. I can't shush long enough or loud enough to get anyone to stop talking so I can find the bottle of ibuprofen.

"Just be quiet!" I squeal.

Those days, when I don't pick up a child on time, and she's waiting on the sidewalk, disappointed and embarrassed.

Those days, when I don't remember how to divide fractions, so I avoid teaching them.

Those days, when I forget to tuck the youngest child into bed because I am engrossed in conversation with another child.

Those days, when I haven't checked enough off my list.

Those days when I've overheard another homeschool mom talk about her child's book-worthy accomplishments.

Those days when my child doesn't answer something correctly a neighbour quizzes.

Those days, when I don't want to hear a child's frustration, so I shut her down.

Those days make me feel like a failure, not good enough.

"A smooth sea never made a skilled sailor," an old English proverb declares. I guess I'm supposed to learn to sail on this homeschool family sea. But I see how far I fall short.

I have one of two choices at this crossroads of self-condemning exasperation. I can continue to be swayed by the onslaught of irritation that comes my way and not do anyone any good. Or I can stop. I can literally stop talking mid-sentence, if need be. Stop trying to force things or figure things. *Breathe.*

I can get to my room, close my bedroom door behind me, sit on a yoga mat, sit in a comfy chair, or stare through the windows toward the river.

I need to listen to what's going on inside me.

Breathe.

What do I feel?

If I sit quietly long enough, my swirling feelings will clarify like flecks of gold in a Klondike's pan.

What is my feeling? I feel like a failure.

In this instance, I should have listened to my child's frustrated feelings and asked more about them. Instead, I tried to shut them down as quickly as they began, because we had other stuff to do.

> Don't define yourself by past mistakes, even if the past was this morning.

I take myself to my bathroom mirror and speak to myself as I would to a friend, "You're going to be okay. These feelings of failure won't last forever. My child is in a stage. She's learning to care about others' feelings. She's trying different behaviours, irritating, unproductive, unhelpful behaviours at times. She wants to see what works and what doesn't. Sometimes she doesn't have words to explain her feelings. She doesn't have clarity about what her frustrations are either. She's more likely to overreact than me, as I've theoretically had more practice. Am I surprised she didn't act maturely? (Well, obviously, yes, I am surprised. I would like her to act maturely all the time, but...) Reality check. So anyway, I'm sorry I behaved in a way I know doesn't work. I forgive myself. Tomorrow is a new day. Or if I want, I can restart today right now."

I speak those words to myself in the mirror. And keep breathing.

All uncomfortable feelings pass eventually, even this feeling of failure.

This homeschool freedom doesn't come for free. This kind of freedom is earned through hard work, mostly the work of the interior.

What is the work?

➢ To acknowledge I have uncomfortable feelings.

➢ To understand why I feel what I feel.

➢ To acknowledge that my feelings need a voice.

➢ To recognize the triggers for my unpleasant feelings.

➢ I must also do the exterior work:

> ➢ Accept my children have feelings unique to them.

> ➢ Accept they don't always know how to identify them.

> ➢ Accept they don't recognize their triggers.

> ➢ Accept they don't always know what to do with their unpleasant feelings.

> ➢ Accept I am a guide for their interior work.

> ➢ Acknowledge they are watching as I grapple with my feelings.

> ➢ Helping my children process their feelings.

There's no manual for parenting, no manual for homeschooling. Okay, there are lots of them; but there are no individualized manuals for our specific children or even for understanding myself.

Therefore, I'll continue to listen to my inner world, learn to listen to theirs, acknowledge uncomfortable feelings, like my failure, right alongside them.

I will keep on keeping on so there will be longer and longer gaps between the days I don't enjoy and those days I do.

I will explore the reasons for the failure. I won't pretend the failure didn't happen. If we ignore the failure, we will surely repeat the failure.

Sometimes, failure compels us toward a new approach. Failure might signal that it's time a child learns something new like his multiplication tables or how to express his frustrations constructively. On the other hand, maybe failure indicates to us that our expectations aren't realistic.

> ...failure compels us toward a new approach.

Don't blame yourself. Girlfriend, no matter your reason, I get you. You had a reason to lose your temper. And yet, there are alternative responses that might be healthier. Your reaction is your responsibility.

What are you going to do now? Acknowledge your failure. Apologize, when required. Ask for forgiveness, if needed. Teach how to do it because your children are not immune to failure either.

How do I not let those failed moments define me? Failed moments inevitably trigger a feeling of shame when I believe I didn't accomplish something I should have. Don't define yourself by past mistakes, even if the past was this morning. .

Failure isn't an identity. Edison didn't discover the lightbulb on his first try. Or the hundredth. He was quoted: "I'm not a failure, I just know a million ways a lightbulb won't light." No one thinks of him as a failure, but he did indeed figure out many ways a lightbulb didn't work.

Let a good night's sleep wash away those mistakes and wake in the morning with renewed purpose. *There isn't a life without mistakes.* Everyone has stories of regret.

"She was unstoppable, not because she
did not have failures or doubts,
but because she continued despite them."
Beau Taplin, *Unstoppable*

Grappling with Impatience

You homeschool. You have children. There are many moments in the day when they need something, and you're sitting in the same room. They interrupt, even though you've asked them not to. Your impatient feelings rise.

What to do? Observe your reaction. Identify what you might say. Identify their response and what they might say. How do you want to respond? If you have ever had a moment in which you said, or at least thought, "I've told you a thousand times," then it's 998 times past the point you could have visualized that scenario, recreated that scenario and planned another way of responding. (I speak from experience: I've said the very thing and didn't visualize my response for 998 times.)

Diffuse tension. Regularly plan to diffuse your tension with short bursts of robust activity: walk around the block, jump on the elliptical or treadmill, do deep breathing exercises, take dance breaks, or run the dog up and down the driveway. Find something you like to do and get moving. Endorphins are your patience facilitators.

Breathe, breathe, and breathe again. I know you don't need to be told to breathe. If you're alive, you're breathing, without intention. But take slow, deep intentional breaths that slow your respiratory and cardiac systems, which slow your fight or flight reactions, which release endorphins, even relieving aches and pains.

Teach your kids mindfulness. During morning circle time or after breakfast, practice patience building exercises. Lovingkindness meditations, prolonged prayers of goodness on behalf of one another, and deep breathing exercises are effective. When the kids are in a peaceful place, there is less conflict. No miraculous overnight transition from sibling rivalry to Zen retreat should be expected.

Observe yourself. Why do you feel impatient? Why do you get frustrated when your kiddo doesn't try to make his cursive as neat as his workbook? We may need to learn about learning and how kids process new knowledge. We might learn our expectations are unrealistic. We might be assuming the worst: "She won't sit down and apply herself; she'll never learn." Or we want to make sure our child sounds like she's at the same level as her same-aged peers.

> Maintain high expectations, but hold them lowly.

We need to observe ourselves. Not judge our feelings as good or bad. We'll often discover some unresolved hurt. Or a presumption that might not be true but is tripping us up.

Interrupt your internal narrative. When you feel impatient, stop, take a deep breath, ask yourself what is getting to you right now? The method we mentioned earlier is useful here. What is the story you're telling yourself that has you feeling impatient? Is the story true? Are you

100% certain your thoughts are true? Could there be an alternate perspective? If your reflection might not be true, if there could be another explanation for the behaviour, perhaps you could approach your thought from a different perspective and therefore, and therefore, elicit a different reaction or response.

Brainstorm five possible outcomes. What alternative ways could you respond?

Act from your best self, not from your reactive feeling. Do the thing you know is the best thing to do. Do that thing from your best person, from the persona you wish to be. **Caveat:** If you're not patient or didn't choose the best approach this time, don't worry, you'll get tomorrow to try again (or possibly five minutes from now).

Is impatience effective anyway? You see a child not doing what you ask, and you show your annoyance. Does impatience accomplish anything more than frayed nerves and further misunderstandings? Impatience certainly doesn't motivate a child. It sure feels instinctive when we see our kiddo stalling when they're supposed to be finishing their French exercises, or getting their writing started, or you fill in the blank.

Maintain high expectations but hold them lowly. I have been told by many over the years that I am a patient parent. This confounds me. (And I don't exaggerate.) My children would be surprised to hear that others think this too. I have pretty high expectations for my kids. Though high is my goal, not unrealistic. I recognize there's a balance between having expectations of my children and not overwhelming them with shame or perfectionism.

Patience is responding slowly under the presence of unpleasant behaviours. I am typically annoyed when one child treats another with unkindness. I have also learned my kids don't mentally process as quickly as I do. I've had to learn they aren't as efficient, or motivated, at doing tasks as I am either. Children are children.

Homeschooling enables patience practice. I've had lots of practice not to be scoldy (still practicing that) and not to yell (do that occasionally too). Twenty-three years into parenting, I'm still practicing. I sometimes stop mid-sentence, walk to my room, lay on my yoga mat and practice deep breathing exercises, walk up and down the driveway, or sit with a soothing guided meditation. Sometimes I'm just impatient.

Patience is the outward practice of understanding someone's unpleasant behaviours. Patience is being intentional in

response to those unpleasant behaviours.

Understanding why someone does what they do, why they think what they think, why they need what they need. Understanding someone is the goal of the relationship.
Understanding forges connection. To identify our struggles in understanding others, we need to define our triggers and preconceptions.
Understanding why we think as we do, what triggers us, and what internal conversations play

> Homeschooling enables patience practice...Twenty-three years into parenting, I'm still practicing.

out in our heads is being emotionally proactive. These actions help us recognize why we find it challenging to understand others.

Identify yourself. Personality profiling, like Meyers Briggs and the Enneagram, have helped me understand much about my kids' strengths and their challenges, how they're internally motivated, and how to encourage them toward essential relationship skills. This self-learning has done the same thing for me. When I understand myself, my natural strengths, my inherent challenges, my natural connections or disconnections with my family members, I relate more smoothly.

Patience sounds like a demanding word that requires our full physical strength and emotional attention. Patience is just this: *understanding another's behaviour.* The more we understand our children, the more we are patient.

Seek to learn about your family members, the dynamics at play when we're not in the room. Seek to understand them when they're with new people, friends, or those other than their family. Seek to learn what others need. Seek to determine who has strong traits in different areas and watch how they can or cannot quickly help each other.

Observe your family members objectively. They are not different from you because they're trying to make your life difficult; they are just different. They are not necessarily trying to challenge you in how you do things; they do things differently.

Practice presence. Mindfulness helps us identify what's happening in our internal world, which helps us manage our external world. Instead of anticipating the future, or planning what needs to be done next, or fretting about how we should have done something differently in some past moment, practice being in the moment right now.

We practice mindfulness for these reasons:

➢ We identify what we feel and become comfortable with uncomfortable feelings.

➢ We recognize our triggers.

➢ We learn to accept ourselves and our struggles.

Acknowledge the feelings and identify why the feelings are present. For reasons that still confound me, the mere act of acknowledging feelings often dissipates their intensity.

Recognize that feelings and thoughts pass through us like weather systems. They come; they go. Sometimes feelings are predictable, sometimes they're not, but an emotional climate always exists.

This practice of being fully present is the most profound therapy available — also, the cheapest. If you haven't tried your vegetables, how do you know whether you like them or not? Try your mindfulness vegetables.

Don't judge your impatience. Be kind to yourself. Your parenting skill has grown by leaps and bounds since you first began. You're learning today. You'll continue to learn tomorrow.

Grappling with Overwhelm

You've got too much to do: too many children to give uninterrupted attention, too many academic expectations, too many meals to make, too many places to drive, conflict with your spouse, irritation with the piano teacher, prepping for a house move, cleaning up after a new puppy peeing on the carpet.

> Be kind to yourself. Your parenting skill has grown by leaps and bounds since you first began.

Time for a breakdown. Instead, break the list down.

Most homeschool families I know have more than one child; however, I have met singleton homeschool families too. Singleton families have unique struggles as they engage and occupy their child most of the time, with no occasional playtime with siblings. Whether you have one child or thirteen, we all have too much to do.

An overwhelmed homeschool mama of five shared: "Our house is very loud, and it feels like we all fall like dominoes once one kid gets started with another."

She explains she has two kids in early

elementary, two in kindergarten and one toddling. She adds, "The noise doesn't help to create a good atmosphere for good learning, so what tricks do you have for peace when trying to teach so many kids at once?" She also says, "We tend to break things into subjects, but something is just not working. I think we're all frustrated; even I'm snappy most of the time. I'm trying to keep things light, but I'm just so frustrated with myself because I can't seem to find what works for these kids. Maybe it's just the winter homeschool blues, but I can't feel good about dragging my kids through each day of homeschool if their hearts aren't there."

Oh, haven't we all been there! I've learned there is no simple solution to any problem. Sometimes the issues stay with us a very long time, either fading out as the child develops, growing parental understanding, or sampling numerous one-size-fits-all solutions that are never one-size-fits-all. Still, all of them seem to help a bit.

Consider these suggestions for the kids' routine:

➢ Change the time of day you do different subjects. Just shaking stuff up can make the day more interesting. History read alouds at the beginning of the day —

math pages at the end. Whatever you did before, do it differently now.

➢ Change the location where you do studies. Give older kids freedom to do studies where they like: on their beds, at a park, in the garage, at the library, or at a café. Permit younger kids to create blanket forts over the sofa, or in the backyard, or bring them to the children's section of the library.

➢ Do a unit study a month. Got a specific topic you're interested in? Spend a month, writing about the subject, research the history, or time period, draw, colour pages, create dioramas, give presentations, create a game, or perform a readers' theatre around the subject. Focus all your study energy on one topic for the month and record all the different ways you have approached that subject so you can see how much you've learned.

➢ Create semesters for different topics. (This is a school solution that surely helps curb boredom.) From September to December, we might select math and science, and from January to May, we might choose history and writing.

➢ Teach history and science together. Unless you're a glutton for punishment or a first-year homeschooler, you don't want to do science and history separately with each of your kids (too much work). If your kids are younger than high school years, they can join read alouds and projects together. They may ask different questions, process things differently, but there are no subjects that can't be understood by a specific age.

➢ Teach the kids separately. A little separate, special time with a parent enables a more engaged and less distractible child. And that child is less likely to irritate her siblings too.

➢ Introduce a new sport. Every season elicits a different sport. Skiing, skating, sledding when the snow flies. Tennis, hiking, and canoeing in the fall. Soccer, biking, and hiking in spring. Baseball, bicycling, and swimming in summer.

➢ Book a scheduled weekly field trip. Somewhere, anywhere, maybe even the library or a café in the town next to yours. Try every museum, every library, every nature reserve or center.

➤ Stop doing everything. Really. Just for a week, or even just a day. Consider this time professional development. Consider this a staycation. Other than not feeding or clothing your child, your children will survive for one week without the luxuries of bedtime stories, afternoon read alouds or extracurriculars. Use this time to take a breather and to gather your thoughts on exactly what is overwhelming you. One day lost does not rock the academic schedule. (And if it does, you should loosen the educational program.)

Here are some suggestions for Mama:

Lower your expectations. Are you expecting every day to be perfect? (Yeah, I know, it's my default too, but perfection isn't a thing, girlfriend.) My reasonable, rational side knows that homeschooling is not bliss. Some days sure seem close though! Some days definitely do not. Perfect is not in a parent's vocabulary. *Good. Good enough.* These are the goal. Really, who is demanding perfection anyway? We know we're neither Google nor God, and we're not training our children to be either. In the wise words of Disney, let it go, let it go…

Loosen the reigns. Remember why you're

doing what you're doing. You have all the freedom in the world. The people you love the most surround you. Take advantage of that. If you haven't already, take a season of unschooling to identify that kids learn despite so many things. Despite the absence of bookwork and academics, despite imperfect teaching, despite the noise, despite disinterest in school subjects, despite conventional methods, despite rubrics, grading, and testing.

> The people you love the most surround you.

Occupy the younger kiddos. Sometimes we need focused time to do specific lessons with older kids. The temporary television babysitter is not evil in short bursts for younger kids and is useful to enable focused study sessions with older kids. A box of Legos, a student basket with craft supplies or measuring cups and a sink full of water (but put away your dish detergent) — whatever works to occupy in short increments.

Don't do as many formal academics. If your kids are young, just read, read, read to them and discuss what you've read. They'll learn so much from this. Follow their curiosities. When a child asks for formal academics or more challenge, explore more learning possibilities. (Some kids never do, but both kids exist.)

Lots of energy is necessary for a large family. I remember someone telling me in my third pregnancy that after three children the parenting efforts were the same. I asked a mom of five to confirm that notion. She said, with a roll of her eyes, "Um, no, a fourth kid is a lot more work." She was right. Be realistic with your expectations if you have more than a few.

It's a lot of effort to homeschool a slew of kids, obviously. Parents with multiple schooled kids are tired too. All parents are tired at times. Parenting with intention is work. Homeschool parenting is around the clock for twenty three years (at least for me). Incredible, rewarding work, but still, work.

We figure out each child and come to understand how to balance what our kids need and what we need as time goes by. Sorry, no quick fix. I won't pretend managing overwhelm is easy. But often, overwhelm occurs as a result of unrealistic expectations.

Either we need to take something off the list, set our boundaries, or sell a kid — your choice. One of those options is illegal. The other two are doable, if only you have perspective and a plan.

One of the biggest hurdles to our peace of mind is *learning how to exist together*. Not every parent is present for their child's twenty-four-hour day. Requiring children to learn boundaries is a lifelong training session. Here are some Homeschool Mama Self-Care needs and more things to consider:

> Time alone. Frankly, whether you see this yet, you need time apart. If you're in your first six months of homeschooling, you may not identify that, however. Just like the wedding honeymoon, there's a homeschool honeymoon. For some, this awareness takes much longer than six months; for some, it's much shorter. Whatever the time, there is always a challenge to find alone time. Alone time, scheduled, in a different location than the kiddos, not just a separate room. No child within sightline or yelling range.

> You need your own thing. Whatever your thing is, it needs to be an all-about-you-thing. Time spent doing something you love to do brings perspective.

> Value quiet. In my observation, the longer a family homeschools, the quieter the children become. I wonder if this happens because parents need separate thinking space when they

are accompanied by children all throughout their day. No matter how hard we try: teaching our family members teaching our family members that we need to think our thoughts without interruption can be challenging. It is a slow process to encourage them to focus on their own work and their own play. Teaching them quiet helps them learn to be attentive to friends and non-parental leaders too. They learn to be empathetic because they listen better. So, it's a win-win for you and them.

➤ Learn to recognize overwhelm. Take yourself to the mirror when you're feeling overwhelmed. Address yourself like a best friend, "Are you okay? How do you feel?" Then accept your feeling, and learn what you need, and where to establish boundaries with your kids. Some days those lessons need to be learned and relearned. Rome wasn't built in a day.

➤ Enmeshment. Recognize that your children's struggles are not yours. You were meant to help them unravel their struggles, but those struggles aren't yours. Though they are our children, they are not us.

➢ You were meant to help identify tools for their challenges, but you can't instill them into their minds until they choose to practice those tools themselves.

Curriculum can often be the source of our burnout. Consider these suggestions for choosing curriculum:

Are you looking for the right curriculum? Good news for you: the search ends here. The perfect curriculum does not exist. Education can be built with snippets of information from textbooks and Wikipedia. Biographies and documentaries detail useful historical study. Apprenticeship positions teach many skills. Solitude and boredom mixed with play, enable creativity. There are a thousand and one ways to build an education. Try them all; expect none of them to create a complete educational puzzle.

Are you searching for a curriculum for a specific child? Remember, you're choosing to educate a child, not a roomful of anonymous children. Keep your child in mind. Halfway through the study season, your child might get bored no matter what. (And so might you.) You may learn that no matter what you buy --

> There are a thousand and one ways to build an education.

books, lab kits, monthly subscription boxes, apps, online educational games, writing classes, math fun books, that you purchased a lot of stuff. You thought it all would be fabulous, but your child did not. Your starting point should be your child, and when it is, you might spend less money. (But they still might not use it fully.)

Pay attention to how your kids approach their learning. Does your child prefer reading independently? Does your child prefer reading together, completing workbook pages, or working on projects at co-ops? Do games help them?

What are his interests? Perhaps he likes dinosaurs. Could he learn to add plastic dinosaurs, subtract dinosaurs, and read about dinosaurs? Does he like to draw dinosaurs? Watch documentaries? Or create dinosaur dioramas? Recognize his interests and incorporate reading, writing, arithmetic, science and history, and you'll see he's getting a thorough education which interests him.

Incorporate your interests. You can include your interests in curriculum choices. Do you like to bake? Bake salty pretzel dough into dinosaur shapes. Do you like writing? Write a dinosaur newsletter to inform the next prehistoric period that the end is nigh. Unit studies of nearly every topic are easy to find online. Incorporate their interests and yours, and you'll keep both your attention longer, and you'll feel engaged too.

Spend a lot of money, waste a lot of money. There's a library around the corner somewhere near you. If you're like many homeschoolers, it's probably your second home. A library card can reduce curriculum expenses. There might be a boxful of curriculum you've stashed somewhere years before and never used — check your own growing home library. Also, there are more online resources than anyone will ever need.

Quell the boredom. Maybe the kids are tired of reading the Apologia Aquatic Animals textbook, and they want to learn a little anatomy. Dip into that. Then, later, if you feel the need to finish Aquatic Animals, return to it. Or don't. You don't have to read every page. Even schoolteachers don't. When you're bored, your kids are definitely bored.

Choose a homeschool philosophy. Let's get to why I'm writing about homeschool philosophies before a haze falls across your eyes as opaquely as the haze of mountain fire smoke settles into my valley every August.

If you're new to the homeschool world, you may have a vague notion of homeschool philosophies. Here are a few: classical homeschooling, Charlotte Mason homeschooling, unschooling, relaxed homeschooling, eclectic homeschooling, and interest-led homeschooling.

I'm sure I'm missing a couple (dozen). There's a homeschool philosophy list a mile long. Choosing a philosophy helps guide your daily choices. Just expect that you learn about yourself, your kids, and learning, too, will affect your homeschool philosophy from year to year.

Your unspoken and spoken philosophy influences how you see your children, how you approach your children's educational goals and their interests. Your philosophy determines whether you tell them they're in a specific grade, whether they get report cards, or whether they have recess. Your unspoken philosophy reveals whether you know who the great Johns are (and I'm not talking about the apostle John, or your John Henry), whether you understand what de-school means, whether you know if Charlotte Mason encouraged nature or screen time, whether you know the Grammar, Logic and Rhetoric phases of learning, or how many pages are in Susan Wise Bauer's famous tome.

You can try all the philosophies, and you likely will if you homeschool long enough. And if you homeschool long enough, you will unearth your philosophy of homeschooling.

Early on, at a homeschool conference, I was encouraged to write a family homeschool philosophy statement each year. I thought, "Oh boy, I don't have time to homeschool everything, let alone write my philosophy statement." As much as I liked writing, the idea seemed tedious.

What was the purpose behind a philosophy statement anyway? It's not like I had time to review a philosophy statement every morning and remind myself whether what we were going to do fit into my philosophy. Homeschool philosophy statements are like a general outline for a book,

> When you're bored, your kids are definitely bored.

or a mission statement for a business, or a budget for a family; random acts of intention won't get you where you want to go. Homeschool philosophy statements direct our practical, daily intentions.

A written homeschool philosophy statement, however, is not permanent. Your homeschool philosophy can change. This is not a marriage vow or a hand on the Bible in the courtroom moment. This is a moment in time when you make a statement of intention toward your homeschool family. A homeschool philosophy statement serves as the energy intended to approach your children, both in relationship and in education.

Then when you are feeling overwhelmed, you can ask yourself: is what I'm doing aligning with my philosophical intention? If so, you can take a deep breath and relax. If not, you can remind yourself again how you want to focus your homeschool.

Your philosophy will change over the years, change with greater awareness of each child, your needs, your children's future intentions, your energy level, and your family dynamics. You'll hone this philosophy for the rest of your homeschool years.

Don't let your best intentions, or anyone else's, get into your homeschool happiness equation. There is no one right way to homeschool. Just as you have learned, there isn't one standard way to educate a child.

My own story of overwhelm:

The first few weeks we homeschooled, we sat

in a circle in July because I was rip-roaring ready to homeschool. (Yes, July.) I rang the bell at 0830 each morning, opened and closed our books on a bell schedule, sat in our homeschool classroom and dictated famous presidential quotes to my writing kids while occupying the preschooler with her activity basket. The 8-month-old baby sat in my lap.

Anywho, that level of structure quickly waned. My homeschool philosophy revealed my philosophy that my children's education occurred because they sat in a semi-circle and a teacher lectured. Someone might call that traditional homeschool philosophy. (Some might call it self-induced torture.)

After discovering John Taylor Gatto and John Holt and devouring everything they wrote, I found my way to unschooling. I became convinced, after watching my children with what I was insisting they engage in- specific topics, but those topics didn't necessarily educate them. If my kids didn't care, they weren't learning. When left to their own devices, they spent extra time playing logic games, creating Barbie storylines, or reading books on undersea animals. Recognizing that kids learn despite a traditional approach, returned life to us all.

I sat with my oldest at a Starbucks on a weekday morning to let her know we would never do studies again. She could do whatever she wanted whenever she wanted. (Secretly, I expected her to delve into atomic theory; instead, she read history books and wrote her favourite Taylor Swift lyrics and taped them to her wall.)

During this time, we traveled plenty, but despite the new venues and numerous field trips, I noticed my three youngest kids were bored. A little routine looked necessary. I gradually incorporated more scheduled activities. Latin and English word roots sounded like a good idea. Learning the French language, since we're Canadian, seemed appropriate, as did learning the Italian language, since we would travel to Italy in the fall. When we travelled to rural Kenya, we brushed up on our Swahili. I taught them a little grammar from First Language Lessons and memorized the rhythmic preposition poem: aboard, about, above, across. We returned to Math U See curriculum: just fifteen minutes a day. And it sure was useful to know a little history and science theory, so I mandated afternoon science or history reading, and required a one or two-paragraph summary of their reading. And then — you can see where this is going — there was always one more thing I wanted us to explore.

We've settled into this schooly-unschooly routine for years now. (Oh, and my eldest, the un-schooler, began University with Latin, German, and History of Roman Civilization. Go figure.)

To plan or not to plan academics: that is the question. I didn't have a name for my style of planning, but I have been enacting this approach almost all my homeschool years: I sketch a routine and include all the elements of an education I want to include, like journaling, poetry memory, writing, spelling & cursive (depending on age), math, Latin and/or French, reading hour, history and science. Sometimes we do geography, economics, logic, and current affairs. My kids' choice of history, science, and writing topics is influenced by their interests and expanded by my interests too. Then we do it. Then we write it down.

When they were younger, at the end of the day, I recorded what we did in a daytimer. As they got older, I had them record their activities in their own daytimer.

At times, I have referred to myself as a classical un-schooler because I dabble in private school subjects, like Latin and Economics. However, unlike private school, the only uniform is pajamas and I don't lecture (well not studies anyway). I certainly don't offer these subjects with scholarly precision, or provide grades, report cards, or scholarships. I have adopted Charlotte Mason's fifteen-minute approach that encourages a tasting of many topics, but we don't sit in those topics long enough for me to get bored (I mean, my kids to get bored). Yet, as the kids got older, I've expected a lot more than fifteen minutes in various subjects.

This approach worked for my three youngest, but not for my eldest child. My eldest didn't want any scripted routine, thank you very much. Even though she was eager to attend public high school, she quickly tired of the expectations and forced the three-year high school requirements in two years. Our second child has been the most academically and routine driven from early on. Our third child recently wanted more academic challenges, which is entirely opposite to her efforts in the past year (they are ever evolving). She is very capable of logic and academics but doesn't always care. Our fourth child loves reading, math, and logic, writes easily, follows along in his older sister's science high school physics, chemistry, and biology labs, and reads history in his spare time. His university-aged sister calls him for Ancient Roman history consultations.

> My eldest didn't want any scripted routine, thank you very much.

I like knowing they're learning and expanding their academic horizons, that they harness their boredom, (and not in the way of screen time free-for-all — I'm not that mom), but I don't need them to learn in a specific way. I'm always on the lookout for skills expansion, like learning to paint a verandah, build a river raft, dissect an old cell phone, or fix burned-out Christmas lights. I also think in terms of community-based learning like computer software classes, chicken husbandry (no, not marrying chickens), and geology field trips.

At the beginning of each year, I plan my plans like an eager homeschool mama. Then I loosely insert them over the study season. I watch for activity overwhelm or underwhelm through the eyes of my child.

Dependent on the child's age, I enable their written communication by encouraging them to write about topics they enjoy. I help them choose a writing focus for each month. First, because that is a reasonable time to complete a writing project. Second, because variety is the spice of life. This might be a research paper, an opinion essay, a newspaper editorial, a free write, a NaNoWriMo project. Then I expect them to engage for a certain amount of time in the morning. A couple times a week, I ask them what they are doing, get them to show their writing project to me, we discuss, and I help them expand so they can be guided in their work.

To curriculum or not to curriculum? We have done Sonlight curriculum (loved it, by the way). Reading is always a good thing and Sonlight has excellent book choices), we have done workbooks, sampled so many curriculums, and have come to understand that not one curriculum is ideal, not one curriculum lasts forever, or not one curriculum works for every child.

I have learned to recognize an educational opportunity outside a lesson plan, textbook, or lecture. The moment when a child asks the difference between a wasp and a hornet. The moments when a child asks me to spell egalitarian. The moments when a child asks to watch the Horrible History DVD series again. The moments when someone asks for help to identify the keys on the piano. Rubbing together two rocks and seeing them crumble in your fingers, then ask why some stones are hard and some are soft. Learning opportunities abound.

Pay attention to the activities and conversations in each of your days, write them down point form, and then you'll be less overwhelmed by the need to plan every moment. The learning moments are already there. You just need to identify them.

One of the biggest hurdles to happiness in the home is simply this: learning how to be together. Yet, we still need to t**ake time alone.** Scheduled. In a different location, not just in a different room. You need your own thing. Whatever that is, this time needs to be about you, without a kid in sight. You need to be on a venture to developing yourself, just like you are helping to developing each of your children.

> The learning moments are already there. You just need to identify them.

Take time to be quiet. In my observation, the longer mamas homeschool, the quieter their children become. Out of necessity, I think. Lots of noise means less of mama being peaceful and able to think. Lots of work teaching the littles to be quieter. A. Lot. Of. Work. Every effort is worth it.

Kids need to be taught boundaries. In a world that often runs counter to this approach, I suggest boundaries are necessary for self-evident reasons. They focus more on their work and their play. They are more peaceful. They learn to be attentive to friends and other adults in their lives. They learn to be empathetic because they listen better.

Kids need to be taught to manage their emotions. They need to learn how they affect others. With kindness and continual efforts (and I mean continual), they will learn what they need to learn. Some days those lessons need to be learned and relearned. Some days are frustrating. Rome wasn't built in a day.

There really is a lot to do as homeschool moms. We might have to learn how to give our children uninterrupted attention. We might have to lower our academic or curriculum expectations. We might have to reconsider why we're feeling overwhelmed and determine that more isn't better. We want to be present in our homeschools and with our kids. Expect that as time goes by, we'll gain clarity what is the "too much" in our days and keep working towards a contented medium. Your family might be a heap load of work but will return its efforts in memories and an abundant life, so keep going girlfriend.

> "You're braver than you believe,
> stronger than you seem,
> and smarter than you think."
> -Winnie the Pooh

Grappling with Loneliness

I find it wild that homeschool moms get questioned about their kids' socialization. Though the homeschool mom is on the move, transporting kids from soccer to choir to curling practice to youth groups, where is the homeschool mom? Homeschooled kids attend many activities every week: co-op, science classes, theatre or piano practice, baseball games, playdates, jobs. Meanwhile, mama is driving, coordinating, managing the house, helping small children, and teaching lessons. Even when there are a few moments, mama is tired at the end of the day, not eager to attend a book club.

She's doesn't feel like asking a friend for coffee or going to a concert. She likes getting into her pj's after a hot bath, then sliding into bed with Netflix or a book, and a bowl of potato chips.

Sometimes mama remembers she hasn't talked to an adult all day, possibly not all week, except in superficial conversations with grocery clerks, post office people, the dance instructor, or violin teacher.

When dad comes home, if a dad comes home, mama wants to talk, and mama has a lot to share. A stable partnering relationship is undoubtedly a valuable part of socialization for mama, but this relationship is not all she needs, and her socialization can't source from just one person.

We homeschool mamas are not alone. We're capable of swimming against the stream. We're willing to do something we're questioned on with regularity. If enough people are asking us questions on our homeschool choice and we have no water cooler to gather around, we might begin to feel like we are alone.

> ...but this relationship is not all she needs, and her socialization can't source from just one person.

We might be one of a few families in our community homeschooling. We might not have a natural connection with other homeschool families. Sometimes, we don't feel we've found our ideal tribe. It's easy to think we are alone in the world.

The notion we are alone is not real, though. Many people from all walks of life experience loneliness, even people who are with other adults all day long. No one is alone in feeling alone.

Loneliness is an uncomfortable feeling. It's a feeling that yearns for an unmet need for deeper connection with others, and sometimes a need for deeper connection with us. Maybe we wish for a relationship that affirms and accepts us in a way we haven't had before. Perhaps we need to deepen our sense of self-value and comfort with solitude. We feel lonely, but are we alone? Seven billion people live on this planet. We are never alone.

Loneliness is a universal human experience. Though we exist within a community of family: long term friendships, community businesses and restaurants, friends and neighbours, homeschool co-op teachers, music teachers, and dance teachers, we are separate and alone in the world. We are alone in this world together.

Other mamas go to work and chit chat in the break room. Other mamas drop their kids at school, have five hours to focus on their projects, but that doesn't mean they're also not lonely. The grass isn't greener anywhere; there are always challenges.

Mama needs to be part of the bigger world, a world that reflects her interests and uniqueness. Maybe she needs a book club for mental stimulation or a dance class to use her body in a creative way. Perhaps she needs to start her own business, take a community college course, or play with a sewing machine. Mama needs her own community that engages her interests.

Your tribe doesn't need to be an ideal group of people. Your best friends might not have homeschooled at all. Your regular coffee dates might not be with homeschool parents. Or maybe they are, but these friends might hold radically different homeschool philosophies.

Recognize the commonality between you and the other person. Just as in a partnering relationship, there are no two people the same, with identical values, identical interests, and identical plans. We pick each friend like a flower in the meadow and make our friendship bouquet. Cheesy, but accurate. There can be beauty in variety.

We connect with one friend in how they parent. We connect with another in our basket weaving habit. With another friend, our paths regularly cross as our kids connect, so our life stories weave together. We find community when we frequently cross paths with anyone as we present our authentic selves.

Practice recognizing similarities. Searching for homogeneity won't work because homogeneity doesn't exist. Look for common interests, common connections, or shared values, but don't expect perfect alignment.

Familiarity breeds friendship. Where you are regularly is where you will make friends. Like the grocery store, pet food store, the library, or extracurriculars. You might connect with your children's 'friends' parents at their playdates.

Try to temporarily set aside your book cover judgment so you can find your connections. Everyone can find commonalities with others, if they choose to look for them. The human experience is every human's experience.

Find friends based on interest. Where to start? Connect where you would go if your children didn't exist. A chess club, an art gallery, or a poetry group? A choir, garden club, or Toastmasters?

There's no guarantee your closest circle of friends are fast friends the first time you meet them, though that has happened to me. Just because you once attended a coding club, a bible study, the gym, or a crochet club, doesn't mean you will immediately connect -

> Mama needs to be part of the bigger world, a world that reflects her interests and uniqueness.

- but you might, over time, so try these places more than once.

Homeschool community is easily available online. In just one popular homeschool Facebook group, there are 11,000 people. I know it's not the same as face-to-face social time. Online communities have their place, and they can connect you to face-to-face people. If eleven thousand people engage in a Facebook group, and we know plenty of homeschool families not on Facebook, then how many more homeschool families are in our face-to-face world, if we seek them out?

You have birthed a community too. Though this suggestion runs contrary to present-day advice, you have birthed, like literally birthed, (or "heart-birthed", adopted) your most valuable community. One day, the kids in your homeschools will probably be your friends. Approach them now as your friends, and you might miss the point of parenting. Though these someday-to-be friendships have a different origin and progression, and you are their prime original social influence, you are making a community of your family.

Overlook your book cover judgment. More than anything, authentically show others your real self. **Vulnerability is required.** Risk being who you really are, not who you think you should be if you want real friendship. This means you need to know who you are, be comfortable in your own skin, and let people know the real you.

Be friends with yourself first. Take yourself to places you enjoy. Not one of my kids will volunteer to follow me into the antique store, but I'm all over that stuff. I'll take myself to a local art walk or classical music concert. I'll eat at the Thai restaurant and order something no one in my family likes. I am different than my family, and I like being with myself.

Brene Brown says it best in her book, *Daring Greatly: How the Courage to Be Vulnerable Transforms the Way We Live, Love, Parent, and Lead.*

> "Belonging is the innate human desire to be part of something larger than us. Because this yearning is so primal, we often try to acquire it by fitting in and by seeking approval, which is not only hollow substitutes for belonging but often barriers to it. Because true belonging only happens when we present our authentic, imperfect selves to the world, our sense of belonging can never be greater than our level of self-acceptance."

As a shame researcher, Brene Brown shares these four powerful elements of true belonging:

➢ People are hard to hate close up. So move in closer.

➢ Speak truth to bullshit. But be civil.

➢ Hold hands. With strangers.

➢ Strong Back. Soft Front. Wild Heart.

Building relationships and connection takes work and requires a lot of intention. We need to step outside our homeschool mama responsibilities and recognize how friendships build our well-being.

Grappling with Perfectionism

With my unique penchants and personality, I instinctively choose perfectionism to gain outward validation and inward affirmation. If others approve of me, I can accept myself. If I've done everything right, I must be valuable. This is not true, but it is my instinct.

> ...I instinctively choose perfectionism to gain outward validation...

Striving for excellence is not perfectionism. Doing a job well done is not perfectionism. Being detail-oriented — st...ill not perfectionism. Perfectionism is the hard pursuit of activity but never feeling something is done well enough. What we do can always be better, so why celebrate and enjoy what we've done? Surely, imperfection is lurking.

Perfectionism in my homeschool comes in the form of trying to squeeze every last drop of life from our days. My morning list might include yoga, meditation, coffee, inspirational reading — all before I've said hello to the kids. Then hug and kiss each child, let out the chickens, check the tiny chicks, feed and water the dog and cats. Bring a daughter to the school bus, another to the transit bus, all before 0830 where I meet my son to do a read-aloud and give direction for math lessons and answer writing project questions.

After lunch, we read from a read aloud, write poetry, and draw or craft, while we watch the chicks toddle around the lawn. All the while, I add to my multiple writing projects. Then I search for writing markets, add to a blog post, an article, my novel, and a poem. Then we move into the travel hour. I transport kids to town, run errands, buy groceries, pick up mail, prep dinner, or make a pitstop at the grocery store for a roast chicken and baguette. I bring the kids home, add to my novel, read, or play games with the kids. I have a meaningful chat with each of my children before bedtime, close the chicken coop, sit with the puppy, chat with my husband, and hope to curl up in bed with a piece of chocolate, two chapters of a book, twenty minutes of tv, then fall asleep. So much activity tells me I have done homeschooling perfectly because I have done so much. Of course, this is not true.

Perfectionism in my homeschool comes in the form of including every clever idea. In our formal academic season, we read together after breakfast, I read history to the kids after lunch, and I read to the kids before bed. If there is a learning opportunity, it must be incorporated. We also draw, study Latin or French, ten minutes of dictation and grammar, and writing projects. I classically school whith an unschooled energy while harnessing my inner Charlotte Mason. There are science and history projects in the afternoons before the extracurriculars. I try to fit every aspect of a private school education into our day.

> I classically school with an unschooled energy while harnessing my inner Charlotte Mason.

Great Expectations could be the theme of my homeschool story. I wring the life out of my days. I expect I'll check everything off my list and when I don't, I am disappointed and irritated.

Answer yes to most of these questions and you'll know you're a homeschool perfectionist too:

> ➢ Do you give up on projects that don't fit your natural aptitude?

➢ Do you spend too much time clipping alphabet printables, hand-lettering, or perusing Pinterest because you know it is the right way to do a project?

➢ Do you double-check your work and the kids?

➢ Do you vacuum your way out of rooms?

➢ Are you continually trying to improve or recreate an aspect of your homeschool?

➢ Does anyone tell you you're spending too much time on a specific project?

➢ Do you avoid trying new activities because you don't want to risk making mistakes?

Is perfectionism the chicken or the egg with homeschool parents? Some homeschoolers go into homeschooling because they feel the pressure to find a perfect stride for their family: the perfect curriculum, the perfect educational philosophy, and the perfect social environment.

What would a perfect homeschool achieve anyway? Our children will learn everything no matter what the educational approach. They'll neither be prepared to replace Google or God.

Are we looking for someone to validate our homeschool? We don't need to impress the grandparents or the neighbours with our clean, organized home and homeschool because they would do parenting and educating differently than us anyway. (The evidence: most of them did.) We need not attempt to Pinterest-perfect our way through unit studies, holiday crafting, or science projects. Someone will always come up with a bright idea for something to which we neither have an aptitude nor budget.

Perfect homeschool SuperMOM has arrived! Declare yourself a homeschooler, and somebody declares their awe. You want to impress with all the wonderful things you do. You share the rundown of your child's amazing academic education and how it meets their interests and aptitudes, and now they only do it in three hours each day.

You also want to be available for late-night chats, never fall asleep in the afternoon for history reading, and you don't ask your kids to help with chores. You can do everything yourself because you know you'll get it completed more perfectly anyhow. It doesn't matter if you get sick, because you have the fortitude to homeschool from your bed still.

You don't lose your temper. You remain calm, cool, and collected always. You love every topic you tackle. You're never disillusioned or disappointed; you enjoy every moment of your homeschool days.

In multi-coloured pens, you track your days and the varied, engaging activities you spent the summer planning. No one gets bored. Especially not you. You never wonder what else you could be doing instead of homeschooling. You never wonder how much income you could be contributing to the household at this time in your family life if you hadn't homeschooled.

You never question your homeschool philosophy. You unschool and let the children direct every hour. You classically school and guide their every step. You Charlotte Mason yourself into an outdoor coop. You unit study yourself into writing and selling your unit studies. You've got this down.

> You can do everything yourself because you know you'll get it completed more perfectly anyhow.

Your weekly housework schedule pinned to the fridge is known and loved by all the kids. They know what to do and when. They wouldn't question you because they know you expect it, and they want to honour you.

You've found yourself a volunteer position. You go beyond your own family's needs and interests and help others in the community and expect your kids to follow.

You make sure the kids have paid jobs. Isn't entrepreneurialism the highest form of industry and the most defining stamp of a homeschool family?

You make sure your schedule remains open for extracurricular driving. Driving the kids to their jobs, their extracurriculars, social opportunities, and the grocery store to feed them fills your evening schedule.

You find the perfect curriculum: a curriculum that enables learning and provides a broad awareness of many subjects.

> Get yourself accustomed to good enough, not perfect.

In your spare time, you brush up your math skills, because you or your partner should be competent in teaching every topic.

When summer arrives, you create cleverly written portfolios, so you know what you've accomplished in the past year (and also so you can write their high school portfolios one day).

Perfect enough? I'd say.

Why are we taking all that on anyway? Are we looking for a bit of approval? *Approve of thyself. Seeking others' approval will be an endless, unsatisfied quest.*

Even if we get awarded a participation badge, a gold seal of approval, or red star stickers for our homeschool mama "Job Well Done," an award still won't be enough. Even if we are invited to every homeschool meet-up and our children are invited to every homeschool child's birthday party, we should socialize our kids more. Even if our learning consultant oohs and ahs over last week's learning opportunities, our parents aren't worried about our kids' socialization, our house is clean, our household budget is maintained, and our marriage is harmonious, even if we don't approve of ourselves, we'll still be searching for validation.

When you can't get over the idea that you're not doing it perfectly, question yourself: How much does what I'm doing matter?

 ➢ What is the worst thing that could happen if I didn't do a task or didn't do it perfectly?
 ➢ Would my children survive their childhood if they didn't get exposed to a topic ever? (You'll probably bump into it eventually).

Create realistic schedules: if you don't complete your to-do list, there's always another day. **Do a time audit:** Charlotte Mason had a bright idea when she suggested doing many subjects in fifteen-minute increments. I took that fifteen-minute notion and told myself if I wanted to do something, I only had fifteen minutes to do it. This practice helped me see how much I accomplished each day. This approach made sure I could get to the important stuff, even for a limited time. It also helped me get to places on-time more often because I discovered how much time everything took. It indeed showed me I had unrealistic in how much I could get accomplished in a day.

> **Set priorities.** Write three things you must do in a day. (That number seems impossibly small to me.) Watch your reaction to the number of things you do. Do you have enough breathing space to complete everything you want to do? Do your kids have access to you too?

> **Challenge one of your expectations.** Show up five minutes late. Let yourself skip a math lesson a week. Don't check a child's spelling book or scrub the toilet for a month. Get yourself accustomed to good enough, not perfect.

> **Assess your to-do list at the end of the day.** Be thankful for your productive day and know that tomorrow will be another day to do more things.

➢ **Put you and your children ahead of your perfection.** Your well-being is always more important than your to-do list, a spotless kitchen, or a tidy minivan.

➢ Lowering your expectations doesn't mean you don't have any expectations. Lowering your expectations means you are likely to accomplish much, recognize the quality efforts you have achieved, and honour the work you have done.

What to do if you're still dissatisfied with imperfection?

➢ Observe your feelings. Why are you feeling what you're feeling?

➢ What is this imperfection story telling you about yourself?

➢ Ask yourself if what you are thinking is true.

➢ Are you 100% certain it is true?

➢ Is there an alternative perspective? How else might you reframe that thought?

➢ Act from your reframed perspective.

➤ Repeat daily affirmations. These help to flesh out who you are and what you want to accomplish in your relationships and your activities.

If you're still struggling with unrealistic expectations, have a chat with a friend, let her know what you're doing today and what you are hoping to accomplish. A little accountability will help.

Above all, accept thyself. Be satisfied with your efforts. Look around and see how your planning has benefited your children. See how your watchful eye identifies organic learning opportunities. See how you're more comfortable in planning menus and managing your household now. See how your temper isn't as turbulent. See how you listen to your kids' more, your marriage is more harmonious, and your home is more enjoyable. See how your children are kind and thoughtful. Good job, mama!

ACKNOWLEDGING MAMA'S INFLUENCERS

We need to choose our influencers wisely

Our thoughts influence our actions and impact our life experience. Our thoughts influence how we make choices in life. It is not just our thoughts that affect us, of course: those around us influence us too. *Therefore, we need to choose our influencers wisely.*

Every person influences us along with our life story. Imagine a theatre stage. We are the main actor. All the world's a stage, Shakespeare says. Each person in our lives is a character in our life story: our parents, children, partner, friends, cousins, aunts, and uncles. Also, the mail delivery person, the café barista, the grocer, the teachers, the employers, the co-workers, the authors of books we read, the coaches of sports team on which we play, the producers of television shows, the musicians to which we listen. These are all our influencers.

The most significant influencers are the ones we allow in our daily lives, not Instagram influencers, not YouTube influencers. Just real people living right alongside us.

The encourager. The bear hugs of warmth after a long car trip to visit Grandma, a warm word from Grandpa on our wedding day, a parent's "I'm so proud of you," or a counselor's encouragement to apply effort in a struggling marriage. Some people pass in and out of our lives, but how the encourager makes us feel lasts forever.

The teacher. The roommate who walked into the room with a warm smile and exuded confidence. The mentor who suggested you didn't have to be afraid in a crowd full of strangers, just be the real you. The independent child that determined she would be happy with or without the approval of others. The teacher teaches without whiteboards and markers.

The nurturer. The one that looked into your eyes and stroked your face when you were sad, that declared you were worthy of being loved, and told you that you have value just because you were created. The one that always responds on the other end of an emergent text. The nurturer makes us feel connected, worthy, and valuable.

The revolutionary. The one that speaks truth without fear. The one that spoke the truth you didn't want to hear. The one that spoke the truth in a roomful of naysayers. The one that convinced and compelled you to practice that new truth. The revolutionary compels us toward truth.

The mirror. The one that makes us see in the mirror something that we need to see in us. The mirror compels us to be honest about ourselves and practicing new skills we would never have accepted if we didn't see it in their eyes.

The villain. The one that knocked the happy out of us whenever she visited. The one that unnerved us with his abruptness. The one that commented on a post unkindly. The villain helps us see what we don't want to be or don't want to associate with.

The co-travelers. Our stories are not the same, but we walk through life with similar stories. We have different scenarios, different characters, but similar themes. The co-travelers remind us we're not alone.

When we are conscious of our influencers we continue to grow and learn and find our way, our purpose, and our impact. Everyone plays a different role. Everyone influences us. Everyone infuses our thoughts with ideas that affect our actions and our experience of life. We must decide who will influence us. Because what we choose to think determines how we act. How we respond determines how satisfied we are in life.

"Watch your thoughts, for they become words,
Watch your words, for they become actions,
Watch your actions, for they become habits,
Watch your habits, for they become your character,

Watch your character, for it becomes
your destiny."
Lao Tzu

Our thoughts today will shape the way we will be living in the future..

My Influencers

There are a handful of people I allow to influence my thoughts on parenting, life, marriage, friendship, creativity, work, and purpose. Some of them are in my real world. Some of them I only know from the published world.

Perhaps I allow them to influence me because I'm searching for answers to things they're answering for themselves. Or maybe it's

> When we are conscious of our influencers we continue to grow and learn and find our way, our purpose, and our impact.

because I have a subconscious awareness that what they're saying is what I know to be true.

These are the authors. They research, then they write their thoughts and their opinions for us to consider. As I sit in the windowed corner of my mountain homestead and underline their impactful sentences, I am the audience that wants to absorb their message. I want to introduce you to the authorial influencers in my world:

- **Gordon Neufeld,** author of *Hold on to Your Kids*. He reminds me that kids live in a peer-based culture, but they never intended to live in the confines of that sterile, impotent circle. Kids were born to be attached and nurtured in the sphere of their parental and familial influences, so they can grow up connected and healthy as a result.

- **Elizabeth Gilbert,** author of *Big Magic: Creative Living Beyond Fear*. She tells me how to let go, create, and commune with the Spirit that seeks to manifest itself in the tangible world. She reminds me to be confident that all my creating has inherent meaning.

- **Sarah Susanka,** author of *The Not So Big Life: Making Room For What Matters*. She reminds me to draw from the simple life, creating space for the essential things. She teaches less is truly more. She teaches that "playing our part in the concert of manifestation, simply experiencing firsthand the brilliant orchestration and choreography of the one who teaches us, our music master."

- **Watchman Nee,** author of *The Normal Christian Life*. The good news of the grace that God accepts us unconditionally before we even decide we want any grace. He declares there's power in knowing that the one who created us unconditionally accepts us.

- **Julie Bogart,** author of *The Brave Learner* and *www.homeschoolalliance.com*. She's the homeschooling cheerleader from the sidelines. She has lived the twenty-year journey of homeschooling, some of those years as a single parent to her five kids. She'll make sure you feel equipped for this journey, challenging your preconceived notions and encouraging you beside every struggle or concern.

- **Brene Brown,** author of *Braving the Wilderness*. She reminds me to stay vulnerable, not respond to shame messaging around me, to analyze why I want to belong at the expense of being the real me, and to stand alone in courage, but also build community by having a soft front, strong back, and wild heart.

- **Brendon Burchard,** author of *The Charge*. He gets me excited about the life I'm living. "The charged life, then, usually calls to us after we have done what we were supposed to do, become who we thought we were supposed to be, lived as we thought we were supposed to live. Then the safety and comfort and compromise get to us, and a stirring of restlessness and revolution sends us off in search of greater adventures and meaning."

- **Eckhart Tolle,** author of *The Power of Now*. He reminds me to live in the now, maintain a practice of existing in the present. "Realize deeply that the present moment is all you have. Make the NOW the primary focus of your life."

- **Dr. Joe Dispenza,** author of *Breaking the Habit of Yourself: How to Lose Your Mind and Create a New One*. Dispenza reminds me that I must take responsibility for my thoughts because they create my world. "Can you accept the notion that once you change your internal state, you don't need the external world to provide you with a reason to feel joy, gratitude, appreciation, or any other elevated emotion?"

- **Rolf Dohelli,** author of *The Art of Thinking Clearly.* "Whether we like it or not, we are puppets of our emotions. We make complex decisions by consulting our feelings, not our thoughts. Against our best intentions, we substitute the question, 'What do I think about this?' with 'How do I feel about this?' So, smile! Your future depends on it."

Atul Gawande, author of *Being Mortal: Medicine and What Matters in the End.* **Gawande eloquently grounds us:**

"In the end, people don't view their life as merely the average of all its moments — which, after all, is mostly nothing much plus some sleep. For human beings, life is meaningful because it is a story. A story has a sense of a whole, and its arc is determined by the significant moments, the ones where something happens. Measurements of people's minute-by-minute levels of pleasure and pain miss this fundamental aspect of human existence. A seemingly happy life may be empty. A seemingly difficult life may be devoted to a great cause. We have purposes larger than ourselves."

You want to know the impact of a writer? It

was Martin Luther who said, "If you want to change the world, pick up your pen and write." For me, the above authors have positively influenced me. I declare, *"If you want to change your heart, pick up a book, and read."*

Be Conscious of You as Your Primary Influencer

Self-care practices can mean spa visits, dark chocolate consumption and Netflix marathons, but when we address our uncomfortable thought patterns, we influence our homeschool world more than anything. Taking time to assess how your own thought life is influencing you can have a beneficial effect on your life and on those around you.

Address your uncomfortable thoughts like a well-argued lawyer. Hold your thoughts to accountability. These self-care practices will help you do just that.

OBSERVE Your Thoughts

➤ Step away & get quiet.

➤ Deep breathe. Allow the slowing physiological practice of intentional breathing brings you to a greater sense of equilibrium.

➢ Observe your interior. Journal your feelings, discuss your feelings with someone, or talk to yourself in the mirror, but figure out what's going on inside you.

➢ Acknowledge and accept your uncomfortable feelings. You're human, so you're going to feel the full gamut of human emotion. You're normal.

RECOGNIZE Your Underlying Needs & ADDRESS Your Feelings

➢ Do your thoughts suggest you need something you don't have?

➢ Ask for help. If you identify underlying needs that could be met by someone else, or determine to set boundaries, then explore how to provide for your needs.

➢ Soothe yourself. When you recognize an underlying need, provide self-soothing practices, like breathing or tapping exercises, talk to yourself in the mirror like a good friend, pray, or meditate.

REFRAME & Act

➤ Journal your intentions every day to remind your how you want to approach your children and your activities.

➤ Question your internal thoughts. Is what you feel true? Are you 100% certain your thought is true? If there is another perspective, what might be its natural outcome if you chose that perspective?

➤ Choose the best possible outcome and act on it.

Gratefulness Practice

Oprah brought gratitude practices to the ordinary person and specifically to me.

Why a gratitude practice works:

➤ Gratitude makes us happier when we practice it regularly.

➤ Gratitude connects us more closely to the people we love. Those we love also sense we're thankful for them. Because we're grateful for them, we're more likely to help them when they need help.

➤ Gratitude reminds us of the happy memories we've experienced.

➢ Gratitude helps us compare less because we are just so thankful for our life.

➢ Gratitude sets us up to believe the future is bright. There is always hope.

➢ Gratitude enables us to be happier with the belongings we already have, thereby spending less on unnecessary things.

➢ Gratitude focuses us on the one who gives us everything we can be grateful for; enabling a richer spiritual life.

Focus on what we do have. Focus on what's going right. Focus on what we've accomplished.

How to facilitate a gratitude practice:

➢ Record daily the things for which you are grateful. Just one thing. Or three.

➢ Write a checklist of the things you take for granted so you can check those things off the list. Health, check. Kids' health, check. Healthy food, check. Clean water, check. Library card, check. Homeschool freedom, check.

➢ Daily repeat affirmations in front of the mirror. *You are beautiful. You are capable. You are worthy.* Whatever you need to hear, so you can listen to what you need to hear once a day.

➢ Share with a gratitude partner. Sharing with a partner builds connection, and every time you say something outside yourself, you are affirming it again to yourself. (They will likely become the one you're most grateful for).

Gratitude practices help steer our thoughts towards contentment and satisfaction in the long term.

In the narrative arc of our lives, we want our days, whether they have good or bad moments, all to have a purpose. Let's practice being appreciative of it all, whether carefree moments or challenging moments.

Honour the narrative arc of your life. Atul Gawande, in his stunning book, *Being Mortal: Medicine and What Matters in the End* says:

"In the end (of life), people don't view their life as merely the average of all of its moments — which, after all, is mostly nothing much plus some sleep. For human beings, life is meaningful because it is a story. A story has a sense of a whole, and its arc is determined by the significant moments, the ones where something happens. Measurements of people's minute-by-minute levels of pleasure and pain miss this fundamental aspect of human existence. A seemingly happy life may be empty. A seemingly difficult life may be devoted to a great cause. We have purposes larger than ourselves. Unlike your experiencing self, your remembering self is attempting to recognize not only the peaks of joy and valleys of misery, but also how the story works out as a whole."

Life is big, includes the good and the bad, and we find purpose when we include it all. Let's be grateful for the good, the bad, and the all.

"You are the single biggest influence in your life."

-Oprah Winfrey

Daily Affirmations for Homeschool Mama

Once upon a time I might have thought it was hokey to recite affirmations. What you say to yourself is what you come to believe. What we believe and think is what we do.

So, on that *thought*, I share recreated affirmations by *mythoughtcoach.com* that encourage me to think as the kind of parent I want to be:

> "I'm a patient and loving parent. I am patient and loving toward myself too.
>
> I'm not bound in any way by my past, or by imperfect parenting I may have received.
>
> I am free to decide what kind of parent I will be.
>
> I completely and fully forgive my parents for any pain their insecurities or unhealed issues might have caused me.
>
> I am guided to the perfect information and resources that I need in each given moment that will help teach and train me to be a better parent.
>
> Every day I am becoming a better person. Every day I am becoming a better parent.
>
> I seek to bring all aspects of my life into harmony. The things in my life that are not serving me, I easily and effortlessly move away from them.

I am moving towards and embracing more good each day.

I wake every morning with gratitude, especially gratitude for being a parent.

I am grateful for each of my children and the opportunities that each of them offers me to become whole and more complete.

I am grateful for those unhealed parts of me that my children sometimes bring out of me because the more I know about myself, the more quickly I can heal and improve.

My home is filled with light and love. I allow this light to flow through me, and in all that we do together.

My home is filled with laughter, with joy, and with celebration.

I know that if I could see each of my children in their fullest potential, I would stand in awe.

I choose, now, at this moment, to have eyes to see them this way.

I take time outs whenever I need them to refocus on who I am becoming and to fill my mind and my heart with light.

I keep my mind firm and focused on what I want out of each situation. I know that what I want is harmony, love, and increasing relationship with each member of my family.

I am preparing my children to become healthy, happy, and capable adults.

I choose to see each of my children in their fullest potential, and as I do, they begin to see themselves that way.

I focus on the good, best, unique in each of my children, and I am their biggest fan.

I discipline with love, never out of anger or rage. I follow all discipline with an outpouring of love.

There is never anything that my children could ever do that would make me love them less.

I seek guidance when I need perspective. And the best information and help comes to me effortlessly.

I am the perfect parent for my children. I am uniquely qualified with what they need most from a parent.

My value and worth as an individual are entirely separate from my children's successes or failures.

I love being inside my skin as a loving parent. This is an expression of my deepest and best self.

I am committed to my own emotional and physical health. And my healing directly impacts my joy as a parent.

I am not a victim of my circumstances. I am free to navigate my course in parenting.

I forgive myself for all the mistakes I have made as a parent.

Each mistake provides valuable information about my healing.

I look to great role models as I move forward as a parent.

I look to God for guidance and direction. I know that my children are not my own.

I take time daily to fill deeply from the wells of truth that surround me.

I am cautious and selective about the materials that I allow into my mind and my home.

My greatest joys are in the walls of my home, where I can smile, laugh freely, and find pleasure in the little things.

I see each of my children as unique and one of a kind. I see within them their fullest potential.

I see myself as unique and one of a kind. I focus not on my past mistakes, but what I am becoming.

I believe in miracles, and I expect them."

MAMA'S BODY

Showers, peeing alone, and other luxuries you can't do with kids under five, feel incredibly extravagant.

Mama's Sleep

Your sleep affects your perspective and your internal world, which influences your external reactions. If you want to help a homeschool kid, mama, get to bed early.

I'm a night owl. My husband is an early bird. This worked great in the early parenting years. I could manage until three in the morning, and he could manage after three. Children do something to your sleep that doesn't feel quite human in the early years of parenting.

As with all things parenting, you learn to adjust, because despite the well-known suggestions in the book, "What to Expect When You're Expecting," kids don't necessarily sleep through the night by four months, one year, or even five years. And if you have more than one child, you could be in for years of sleep disruption.

You're looking after the basic needs of your kids. You ask them to brush their teeth, put on their pajamas, and tell them, "No, you can't have the iPad in bed with you, but yes, you can read before bed." You might pray with them before bed, say a blessing, sing a song, turn on a meditation or Audible book offering and kiss them goodnight. They know to expect their bedtime routine. You know the importance of a sleep routine for your kids. You need that bedtime routine for yourself too. Once upon a time, we were those children needing encouragement to do those very things, and we still are.

Get to bed before midnight. My husband, a physician, was taught that every hour before midnight is equal to two hours of sleep. It was his Grandma that taught him, not medical school. I don't know about you, but I know I feel a whole lot less rested if I'm going to bed after midnight. And I have known that truth for years, but I still find it challenging to get myself to sleep at a reasonable time because I want quiet time after the kids. As the kids get older, and go to bed later, I want quiet after them. Only then do I feel able to free-range an hour by myself.

Nonetheless, no matter how enjoyably I while away my evening alone time, sleeplessness translates into challenged moods.

Sleep deprivation is the ultimate shock of motherhood. Am I supposed to survive on this little sleep? Remember when you were pregnant with your first baby, and other mamas told you to get your sleep because you'll need it? You thought to yourself, "They don't understand how sleep deprived I am as this baby grows inside me. I can't move without stomach indigestion or nausea, or someone pounding me from the inside while I'm trying to fall asleep. Or, I'm so excited I can't sleep. All I do is dream about who this little one is inside me, plan for his perfect little nursery, and our wonderful family life. Yet, I'm told I need to get as much sleep as I can get?"

> You know the importance of a sleep routine for your kids. You need that bedtime routine for yourself too.

Fast forward three months, and you are initiated into the world of acute sleep deprivation. How am I supposed to function if I wake every two hours for an hour to feed, change, and soothe this little one?

No time to answer that question as you move into the second year of your first child's life, and then introduce a new baby again. That sweet, addictive baby smell, those tiny little hands — introducing another little being into the world is such bliss. So, time to start again. And so it continues until your family is complete.

When the early childrearing phase turns school-aged, when you can't remember the last time you didn't sleep through the night, when your oldest child pours bowls of dry cereal with milk for each of her siblings, and when you can snuggle in your bed till 7, you realize you've made it through the most sleepless part of your parenting years. (Yet, they still occasionally sneak into your bed with you.)

> Homeschool is a satisfying life, but it's not a glamourous life.

I know your house is a mess, you need to put a fresh hand towel in the bathroom, put away the dishes before lunch prep, write your weekly menu plan and grocery list, but you're tired. I know you feel the need to get consistent with the kids' studies and get into that new curriculum already, but you're tired. You need to take a nap.

On the other hand, relieve your brain of your

high expectations, let your brain recharge and REMify, and let a nap do its work. Allow your perspective to shift. All you need is a good ol' fashioned nap. Those dishes will get done when your partner is home, or you can buy a stack of paper plates.

Nap when you can, whenever you can, especially if you're in a demanding phase of parenting, or even if you're just plain tired. Napping is an easy prescription to enable perspective.

Create a basket of activities for older kids to occupy themselves with while you and the youngest kids nap. Just fifteen minutes. Everyone can hang out in their beds or cribs. Even if it's just a training ground for a quiet time, fifteen minutes can do wonders.

Vitamins and natural supplements can enhance the quality of our sleep as well. The magic of the magnesium supplement found in the natural food aisle is its ability to secure sounder sleep. Magnesium is not a sleep drug. It also has the potential for diarrhea if you take too much. But Magnesium can aid sleep, though.

Maintain a healthy sleep routine. If you are challenged with sleep issues, sleep experts suggest creating consistent bedtime routines and waking yourself at the same time every morning. Your body will eventually adjust to the wake time, and you will want to fall asleep earlier. Also, eliminating blue light such as screens prior to bedtime helps one fall asleep more easily. Perhaps a real paper would help wind down your brain better than Netflix.

"Take sleep seriously...it increases attention, concentration, intelligence, and health."

Dr. Caroline Leaf

Mama's Grooming

In my early parenting years, I was a poster girl for the hippie movement. I didn't know it, though. I bathed as infrequently as I could get away with, brushed my teeth to keep the dentist away, and decided not to spend money on make-up when I could spend money on baby clothes instead. At the time I thought I was being lazy, but I know now I was overwhelmed. The first baby switched my gears from a slow fourth to an eager first in the drive between the hospital to our home.

Once I had two more babies, I saw that if I didn't make essential grooming a priority, I would spend a lifetime without smelling presentable.

A shower a day keeps depression away. Nothing

statistically supported in my statement as far as I know, but there's something to be said about feeling good in our physical bodies. Bathing scrapes off the cobwebs of haziness and prepares us for the day. *Everyone's version of grooming is different, but when we feel presentable, we feel present for our day.*

Enable the wardrobe. Over the years, my wardrobe has grown in yoga pants and cozy t-shirts like Lego blocks under beds. My wardrobe goes from bed to kitchen, to car and off to dance lessons, then the grocery store. Homeschool is a satisfying life, but it's not a glamorous life.

What I usually wear is some form of comfy yoga pant and sweatshirt until lunchtime, and if I'm heading to town, dark wash skinny jeans and a button-up blouse. If I spend any time doing projects outside, planting the garden, running after a stray garden-eating chicken, or walking the puppy, I dress in grubby jeans and long-sleeved shirts. You won't experience fashion-envy befriending me.

I am no poster girl for any fashion movement. I've tried all sorts of styles through the years, but my ideal wardrobe is a combination of 1940s floral dresses and the present-day Banana Republic preppy. I've sampled the Lulu phenomenon, but I don't have the backside to support it.

Still, find a fancy wardrobe. I know you're likely to default to your yoga pant collection or join the kids with their pajama outfits. Undoubtedly, I lead the pack in yoga pant collecting. Choose clothes that reflect you beyond your homeschool existence, and find reasons to use them.

Showers, peeing alone, and other luxuries you can't do with kids under five, feel incredibly extravagant. Eye cream sounds as luxurious as monthly spa visits. No doubt, grooming is a challenge with wee ones underfoot. Be encouraged: this too shall pass. Eventually.

Learn to build up a resistance to your kids' cries. (Yes, I'm saying that.) There's a balance between addressing your personal needs and your young child's needs. I'm all for responding to kid's needs, but the benefit of a shower on a sleep-deprived mama is underrated. Either ask a family member to look after the kids, pay a young neighbour, or practice listening to the child's cries for a few minutes while you continue to lather.

Shower in the morning is optional. Back when I just had a husband and no children, no one needed to tell me to have a daily shower. But have a shower in the morning with kids? Inconceivable. I have stuff to do. I leave that cleansing routine for evenings, with a lit candle and bubble bath, massaging my head with a mint-fragrant shampoo. Then I slather my legs and feet with lotion before I tuck them into fluffy socks.

Schedule cheap spa visits in your home spa. Once a week, take a spa visit in your bathroom. Bubble bath, cut your nails, paint your nails, face mask, aromatherapy oils, and candles, maybe a glass of wine with a book or some beautiful music, and Calgon take me away.

If you've got small kiddos and are wondering if you can be in the bathroom alone for two whole minutes, I feel you. I remember that like yesterday. (It was yesterday, and my daughter is eighteen). Try to occupy your younger kids while you're busy, continue to teach them your boundaries, and soon enough, you too can brush your teeth twice a day and sit on the toilet in glorious peace.

Just a few minutes is all you need to wash your face with a cleanser, spread eye creams around your eyes, brush your teeth to decrease dental bills, and brush your hair into a headband or ponytail. *The upgraded facial care routine: make-up, facials & make-overs sound divine, not that I have time.* Call me a skeptic, but I don't think those eye serums reduce your fine lines enough for us to look a year younger than our actual age. I am getting wrinkles with or without fancy eye cream. Still under my thirteen-year-old's passionate influence, I finally bought an eye cream. Whether eye serum reduces fine lines or removes age spots makes me look the same age as my teenagers, it doesn't matter. These activities feel self-nurturing because they require me to stop and smell the rosewater spritz as I meditatively tap my face.

I only learned about these products when my third daughter booked us facials and make-overs at a high-end make-up shop for her thirteenth birthday. She wanted me to have a makeover. This facial booking committed me to pay for product. Wow, was it worth the expense? I am still not convinced these products will have a wrinkle breaking, face glowing, dark spot lightening, age-regressing effect. But it felt great.

> ...soon enough, you too can brush your teeth twice a day and sit on the toilet in glorious peace.

These activities make me feel like I'm taking care of myself. Almost with meditative effort, I scrub that facial cleanser in light circles, swirl eye moisturizer on undereye circles, rub that whipped daily moisturizer across my frown-lined forehead and know I have done my age-defying deed. And if there's an age reducing, skin moisturizing benefit to my routine, all the better.

As for super mama grooming, like wearing make-up, we're not looking to Kardashian-ize our homeschool mama identities, but sometimes a little face colour brightens us. I bought an expensive Christian Dior lipstick in high school. I haven't needed to worry about replacing it because I still have that lipstick. There are only so many places you can wear a shade called Mannequin. Instead, I have used the same make-up routine since watching *The Young and the Restless* with my afterschool babysitter in the 1980s. I loved how the actresses' eyeshadow flared at the creases. Shades of brown and dusty pink lipsticks were the television trend. I still like those shades and have been doing that make-up routine ever since. We'll call this my signature style. Make-up is a personal choice. Being comfortable in one's own skin is not.

"When it comes to your body, love the one you're with."- Dove

Mama's Morning Routine

I need quiet in the mornings to start our homeschool days. It sets my day in a chosen direction, rather than a reactive direction. It gives me a little time to think about how I want to approach the day and what I want to include in the day.

Homeschool mamas of younger kids, I know what you're thinking: say what? is quiet time a thing? You wake and hit the floor running. (Or you already have a kid tucked next to you when you wake, so you can't even run). Morning quiet time will arrive in your world. It has yet to arrive on your doorstep and I promise quiet will come.

Some days feel like a whirling dervish. I began parenting with a colicky baby who didn't want to sleep, who tried to feed all the time, cried most of the day, and never wanted to be put down. Then I had three more kids, four kids under seven years (a declarative statement about my will). I wondered if I would ever pee alone again. I wondered if I would ever sleep with just my husband again. That took fourteen years, but it finally happened.

- ➤ **Gradually carve in morning time,** aka insist that mommy really does want you to play by yourself and be quiet for thirty seconds, then one minute, then five minutes, and you will eventually find your morning quiet.

- ➤ **Here are my top five quiet activities each morning:** journaling, inspirational reading, yoga, UV light in winter, and meditation. (Assuming I've also taken care of grooming basics.)

- ➤ **Cave coffee:** put that coffee maker on a bedside table with a couple mugs so you can roll out of bed before the kids discover I'm awake. (Or if you're so lucky, plant your master suite near the kitchen as I did). And sit back for just fifteen minutes to savour your quiet time. (And if you're not yet drinking coffee, kudos to your supermom-ability). If you can't do caffeine, a hot drink is useful as a comfort tool nonetheless.

➤ **Inspirational reading** influences how you think by listening to thinkers other than yourself. Pull out a book on something homeschool encouraging, like a Julie Bogart or Sarah Mackenzie offering, or something mindset challenging, a scriptural reading, or a book of prayers. Choose to get inside someone else's head and learn from them: so many books, so many blogs, online resources, and wise people who have gone before us.

➤ **Yoga:** better stretch that body, before you start doing deep knee bends to pick up heal-stabbing Lego pieces off the floor. Keep those muscles limber.

➤ **Meditation helps me learn my interior world.** You can do this alongside a yoga routine, as you listen to your breath, or use someone's online guided meditation to get you quiet.

➤ **Journaling**

When I was seven, I bought a locked green journal with my first weekly allowance. I printed with a 2HB yellow pencil and wrote the same first line for years: "I woke up, I made my bed, I brushed my teeth." Deep stuff.

As a teenager, I wrote about my dreams for the future. I've journaled about parenting and marriage, friendships and family relationships, my feelings, my days' activities, and my plans, my goals, and my intentions.

Journaling also helps me know my interior world. When we practice this for years, we more easily identify our thoughts and feelings. We can be honest about our feelings, consider whether they're true, or not, and determine how we need to engage them, or whether we engage them or allow them to pass. Journaling is a helpful tool to get everything outside us and in front of us for consideration.

When we journal for years, we discover that we think similar thoughts on repeat. There's not nearly as much variety in our thought lives as we might imagine. Journaling makes it easier to identify what thoughts aren't working for us. We need to change our mental approach. Sometimes journaling helps us identify that certain situations aren't working for us. We need to change our situation. Maybe we've sat long enough in a situation we need to get outside perspective.

Journaling reduces stress. Just as having a friend listen to our unpleasant feelings helps to decompress them, so does "Miss Journal". We don't have to give our journal a name, but that might help. Seeing our journal as a separate person might help us to be more open. We gain the benefits of a trusted, nonjudgmental friend.

Journaling encourages gratitude practice. Being grateful for what we already have and being grateful for how life is progressing helps us have forward-moving potential. Being grateful doesn't come naturally. Naturally, we focus on what's going wrong, what could be better, what we could do differently, or what others could do differently.

Take care of your morning and take care of the rest of your day.

Mama's Fitness

Sometimes we scurry back and forth between one child and another at the kitchen table. Sometimes we're running to the newly walking toddler to prevent her from falling down the stairs. Making meals, washing laundry, sweeping floors, helping kids choose the right word for their story, asking kids to narrate history readings, or driving to extracurriculars: these activities occupy us but they don't facilitate natural exercise. If only we had leg-powered Flintstone cars.

None of us has extra time to exercise. However, if world leaders can fit it into our days, we homeschool mamas can too. If exercise isn't already scheduled into our routines, we are declaring, "Exercise isn't important to me." (PS I feel you. It's not my instinct either.)

Of all the things I wanted to do as a child, playing tag on the playground or playing on a team weren't my chosen activities. Since I grew up being influenced by someone who controlled her weight as a source of control in her life, the subtle messages about diet and exercise spoke volumes: fine-tune your body to be picture perfect.

> I still would rather focus on regular activity than my physical vanity project because exercise has so many intrinsic benefits.

In high school, I didn't know my five-foot eight-inch, 130-pound body was of model proportions. I saw myself as too big. I spent my teenage days counting the number of Oreos I consumed. Then I considered how many minutes I would need to stay on the stationary bike to burn off those Oreos. Hollywood values of vanity and image infused my high school goals.

Then I had babies and an anorexic mindset was no longer my issue. I carried a couple babies around my midriff after my body no longer housed them. I enjoyed pregnancy gain: all those pizzas, ice cream, iced cappuccinos and A&W chubby chicken burgers. After my youngest was a few months old, I huffed and puffed as I walked up the staircase of our second storey home. Trying to reclaim my pre-born pregnancy body while I craved and consumed Chubby Chicken burgers was a challenge. However, I tired of my fatigue, so I got myself into our basement while the youngest napped and increased my fitness on the most boring place on earth, the treadmill.

I didn't get to my runway model status after I began regularly exercising. I wanted to walk up the stairs without stress. I still would rather focus on regular activity than my physical vanity project because exercise has so many intrinsic benefits.

➢ **Exercise provides nature therapy.** Getting outside does something for our souls. When I walk along the neighbourhood canal with my dog, I enjoy the snow-rain that weighs down the limbs of the cedar, larch and Douglas fir trees, the mountain view, and the sight of the canal holding back the river. I see bald eagles and beavers slapping their tails against the river. When I get to walk outside, I get physical activity and enjoy the ambiance I was built for, the great outdoors.

➢ **Exercise supplies endorphins.** Dopamine and norepinephrine are what my brain is after. I don't enjoy a sweaty public gym, home gym equipment, exercise DVDs, or weight benches. No thanks. One thing the home gym does though: it gives me no excuse when the weather is not agreeable. Even if it's just fifteen minutes. Fifteen minutes to enable endorphins to surge through my body to energize mind.

➢ **Exercise builds family connections.** Once a year, we participate in a city-wide run. This activity is not my cup of Gatorade. I am not that mom, running competitively. (Though I have that friend. Apparently, it's not enough just to know someone who runs marathons). The memory of running up Doomsday Hill with my nine-year-old son is priceless. "Keep going," I encouraged, and he did. Sweet memories.

➢ **Exercise burns general tension.** Homeschool mama's days are jam-packed with voices and energy. Burning off steam and building physical resilience is useful when you're chasing young kids at the playground. Also, when spending a lot of time addressing a teenager's emotional management skills. Burn off tension? Every homeschool mama needs this by arsenic hour (dinnertime). Somehow, someway, every day. (Or at least, most days).

➢ **Exercise manages your weight.** I know you already know this. If you're looking for an exercise/diet regime that will help you lose weight and be as cute on Instagram as the Kardashians, I'm not your girl. Consistently exercise at least three times a week for a half-hour and eat within the dietary guidelines for your age and height, and you will likely maintain your present weight. Increase your exercise effort over time and feel better. That is all.

➢ **Exercise diminishes premenstrual tension.** PD days, Professional Development Days at schools, don't exist for homeschool mamas. It might be wise for homeschool mamas to honour PMS days though. Tracking our periods is useful for our self-awareness and family happiness. My family knows when I buy a bag of potato chips or peanut M+Ms, I am near that date. Exercise decreases the irritable, emotional tension that arrives with the bag of M+Ms.

➢ **Exercise increases energy.** Weird, but true. Expending energy through exercise begets energy. Exercise is one of those gifts that keeps on giving.

➢ **Exercise improves focus.** You're going to be more easily able to focus. This is necessary when you're trying to expend your energy in so many different directions.

➢ **Exercise decreases long-term health risks.** You're likely not thinking about this yet, but how to offset dementia? Experts say: exercise.

➢ **Exercise builds your core.** Find Pilates workouts or do planks, bridges, superwoman exercises (might as well do the official ones, as you're doing the unofficial superwoman exercises anyway). Do core exercises in proper form to prevent back and neck pain.

How to start? if you haven't got a form of exercise included in your days, might I suggest the following:

➢ **Buy exercise clothes.** (Yeah, I know, I'm not that girl either.) Wear them in the morning till your workout is complete and you'll be wearing an easy reminder.

➢ **The fifteen-minute rule: d**ecide how you want to get active for fifteen minutes. If ten minutes in, you can no longer breathe, and you're pouring sweat, stop and try again tomorrow. Your goal is just fifteen minutes, three times a week. Even if you can do just five minutes, start with five. Keep building.

➢ **Do what you love.** Don't do the elliptical if you hate exercising on machines. If you like aquafit, nature hiking, canoeing, or swimming laps at the pool, start with that. Did you play volleyball before the kids were born? Play on a ringette team? Squash on Saturday mornings? Do what you like. Don't do stuff because the activity is trendy, because you won't sustain that behaviour.

➢ **Do it together.** You can do all sorts of activities with your kids: yoga, calisthenics, videos. Do you own a trampoline? You will learn how much exercise the kids get when they are on that contraption.

➢ **Think seasonally, if you live in seasons.** As I mentioned earlier, skiing, sledding, snowboarding, cross country skiing, and snowshoeing in winter; swimming, hiking, canoeing, biking, and tennis in summer.

➢ **Do it alone.** YMCA or local gyms may have childcare options. When your partner walks through the front door, say hello and put on your walking shoes. No guilt, no shame. Or if you drop your kids off at the YMCA playcare or exchange your kids with a neighbour once a week, no guilt, no shame. If you enjoy your hour of quiet exercise at a gym, lifting weights, swimming laps, or joining aquafit classes, do your thing. Everyone is happier when you're happier.

➢ **Build a community while exercising.** If you remember those pre-children activities you did with your group of friends, like floor hockey, tennis, or competitive swimming, find a group. The group will keep you going.

➢ **Plan a fixed time.** If you're not a morning person, and you're pretty sure your body doesn't do those movements until after lunch, don't. Exercise whenever works for you. Then write your plan into your phone with an alert. **Just three times a week.** Then work up to an activity every day. You probably won't be consistent, but when you assume exercise as a regular part of your routine, you'll remember more often.

What to do? I share a few ideas here, but I'm sure you can come up with a few without me.

➢ **Strength training twice a week.** Just as your children grow up right before your homeschool mama eyes, you also grow muscles, not for fancy Insta photos of you besting your last barbell lift, but because you want to walk up your front steps with bags of groceries when you're eighty.

> Consult with your physician before following any advice of a medical nature

➢ **Create a Spotify family dance list.** Dance around the living room with loud music. Dance will get your heart rate going, burn off everyone's tension and add a little happy, especially if you're dancing to Pharrell's "Happy" for the zillionth time.

➢ **Yoga.** Poor misunderstood yoga. Do yoga just fifteen minutes a day and discover you are stronger, more grounded, and calmer throughout your day. Yoga's anti-inflammatory effects might put the NSAID industry out of business if everyone stretched and strengthened into yoga positions every day.

➢ **Aquafit.** Yeah, I know, you're not that old. However, I assure you, a workout in the pool is enough exercise, uses every muscle known to your body, and feels refreshing, minus the sweaty effect. And unlike running, your body will never tell you that you're too old to swim.

➢ **Dance.** I bring my girls to a half dozen classes a week, each daughter, times three daughters. That's a lot of dancing. But I don't see the inside of the dance studio. I would love to fit in just one class a week. Whatever they're doing, we can too, right?

➢ **Get a dog.** That lil gal will require some attention, require you to get up and get her going. Put up a schedule for regular dog walking each morning or afternoon, for the kids! And add yourself to the list. Research suggests that outdoor time slows your heart and respiration rates.

➢ **Schedule daily homeschool gym class.** No, you don't have to call it gym class, but the kids need exercise too. Have you tried Wii dance videos, basketball, tennis, beach volleyball, baseball, football, or soccer? A few minutes together in the middle of a study day to burn off some tension.

➢ **Think recess.** I know you're a homeschooler, and you don't need to think in school terms. Think outdoor exercise break instead. The beauty of living alongside your child's daily routine year-round is how quickly you learn your children can't sit at the kitchen table for three hours consecutively. Many mental breaks are healthy.

➢ **Take up outdoor activities.** I happen to live in a small town where I experience positive peer pressure to be active outside. If you don't live where I do, consider weekend trips experiencing canoeing, fishing, boating, swimming, hiking, or nature walking. The mixture of nature and exercise is proven effective in benefiting our brains and our happiness.

So, let's get moving!

Mama's Nutrition

I'm of the opinion that most North Americans could teach a nutrition class. We've been taught, we've been told, and we know how to eat properly.

We're running the kids from dance class to choir, and we pass by a burger joint and think,

"Dinner prep and clean-up would be so fast." We are exposed to what we know is good for us, but the convenience makes our choices challenging. Prepared food is fast, but prepared is not often brain-nourishing food. When we feed our brains the best fuel, we function at our optimum. **Plan in advance.** Get food containers for each family member, and a list of foods that can be prepped for a few days, that include a protein, vegetable, healthy fat, and carb.

Eat from the rainbow. The American Cancer Society recommends five to nine servings of fruits and vegetables a day. Eating from the rainbow is a great way to think about healthy fruits and vegetables. Strive to eat red things: strawberries, raspberries, cherries, red peppers and tomatoes; yellow things: squash, yellow peppers, bananas and peaches; blue things: blueberries and eggplants; purple things: plums and beets; orange things: oranges, tangerines and yams; and green things: peas, spinach and broccoli.

Here are easy ways to include the rainbow every day:

> ➢ **Start your mornings with green smoothies:** spinach, banana, almond milk and berries. If you're feeling wealthy, include green supplements like chlorella

and spirulina. When you start your day with a pre-blended drink, you spend little time in the kitchen, and you start your brain with high-octane fuel that feels great.

➢ **Preplan snack times**: an apple and nuts or hummus and veggies. These are easy to grab.

➢ **Assume** that half your dinner plate is **filled with vegetables**. Think simple diet, simple life.

➢ **Teach the kids to cook.** Learning to cook encourages kids to sample their product and eat with a little more variety (ok, well, some kids...some kids won't eat the fish just because they prepped the fish). Build food preparation into your family culture, and you will expand your repertoire, and sometimes, their interests might expand yours.

Supplement your diet: my husband, a medical doctor, is a skeptic about supplements because research suggests many supplements, even Vitamin D, are not used effectively by the body as we once hoped they did. And yet, I feel a whole lot more energetic with a B complex vitamin, and I see how some of my kids don't prefer their rainbows, so I'm all over vitamin supplementation. I take a host of supplements that increase my overall sense of well-being. Dr. Daniel Amen is also a medical doctor that shares excellent resources about brain health and brain supplements. What better thing for self-care than to take care of our brains?

Be moderate in your dietary expectations and avoid fad diets. I've not eaten a raw diet, except for occasional sashimi at Japanese restaurants (which is fabulous). I did sample a low acidity diet: I purchased alfalfa but didn't supplement garden soil or farm animal feed. I fed alfalfa to myself in smoothies and tried to feed it to my kids too. It was surprisingly expensive, and to no one's surprise, the kids wouldn't eat it. That fad diet didn't catch on for obvious reasons. As a teenager, I was exposed to crazy diet books and schemes through the eighties and nineties. We had an unhealthy exposure to spandex, aerobic videos, leg warmers, runway models, diet drugs, and spot-reducing exercises.

Current diet fads have changed: eat your kale and quinoa! Fermented foods are all the rage. Sauerkraut pickled green beans, dilled carrots, water kefir, apple cider vinegar, and sourdough breads are part of my healthy diet because I like to live old fashioned on purpose and make meals at home. I've learned they're also excellent gut-healthy choices, so this is a diet trend I can embrace.

I have learned healthy eating is a self-loving practice. Just like insisting our kids eat their veggies because their brains need to be fed, not just their mouths, I try to include increasingly healthy choices too. I can see the value of healthy eating, but sometimes it is hard to maintain.

Things I'm learning about healthy eating:

➢ I can change my cappuccino morning routine to an Americano (no milk), or even, gasp, a rice milk infusion if I need to exclude dairy from my diet. I can switch to Yerba Mate tea or green tea if coffee is an issue.

➢ Most prepared foods have added sugar. Sugar is an inflammatory substance we are wise to avoid, so the less sugar the better.

➤ Less fast food means more nutritious food. Our town has kept major fast food options out, so this option is not easily accessible. And I live far enough out of town that ordering in would make the takeout drivers giggle: "You live where? Yeah, we don't drive there." Homemade food is more effort, but mostly healthier.

➤ A yummy substitute for butter on toast: homemade cashew butter and fruit compote. Toast without butter is an adjustment, whereas quinoa with a sprinkling of cocoa nibs, berries, and coconut flakes is satisfying. There are delicious alternatives to toast with butter.

➤ I have learned to lighten my meat consumption with beans, eggs, and tofu recipes. These are easier on the checkbook and digestive system. Broiled chicken is still divine in my mouth. Baked halibut and fish tacos are regulars on our dinner plates. Once a month, I require a serving of cow to keep the anemia away. Twice a week, meat consumption is vegetarianish for me.

➤ Fermented foods are a palate alternative to my potato chip addiction. A green olive, slosh of sauerkraut or tangy, garlicky pickle are a salty, crunchy alternative to my Miss Vickie's preferences.

➢ Soda streams are a useful approach to getting more fluid. Fizzy water, yum. **Put it in a wine glass and enjoy the experience more.** Buy a water bottle with your name if it gets you drinking more.

➢ Pecan crackers with avocado slices and pepper flakes is a yummy, crunchy late-night snack.

➢ **Don't annihilate treats.** Chocolate is good for us too. Daily magnesium supplements provide similar benefits that chocolate provides and helps us sleep better too. (But chocolate is tastier.)

➢ **Drink alcohol sparingly, but intentionally.** A glass of wine preparing dinner on a weekend evening, listening to a cooking show, enlisting the kids in food prep with their glass of Fresca is a lovely way to enjoy the weekend. I love Barefoot Contessa because I love her kitchen and her garden. Choose a favourite cooking show

Eating healthy in our indulgent culture requires God-sized self-control. Eating whatever we feel like is just too easy. We live in a culture of palate-amusing food options at every turn. No time to get bored, lonely, sad; instead, eat something. I'm learning to choose foods that are not necessarily my palate-preference, but I've learned my palate follows suit when I intentionally change my diet. Brain health is my goal and nutritious food enables a happy homeschool mama brain.

Mama's PMS Days

Once upon a time, when I was in grade 5, I was excited about a special class. Mom had to sign a permission slip for me to attend. There was much talk at recess about this class. This was a gender-separated class with information about female anatomy, the menstrual cycle, and brochures for feminine hygiene companies.

I was excited about becoming a woman. (Roll your eyes, but I was genuinely thrilled.) I would decide one day whether I would buy Kotex or Always. I was told that one day soon, I, too, would wear a bra, so every night after that class, I asked my mom if I was big enough for one of those flat pink starter bras. (Yes, I really did.)

Fast forward a decade, or three, and the initiation into womanhood has lost its bloom. I've had four babies, five pregnancies, and Kotex and Always are as regular items on my to-buy list as apples and bananas. It's far easier to focus on the negatives of the premenstrual experience for obvious reasons. It interferes with my regular routine and can be emotionally challenging.

Women are blessed with the privilege of bearing children, nurturing children, and experiencing the seasonal monthly shifts of emotions. We feel elated when our babies enter the world for the first time and are placed in our arms for nurturing. Still, there is a

> ...I can't call anyone to replace me for a sick day...

remarkable responsibility not to rip into that very child when we are dipping to our lowest emotional ebbs in our monthly cycle.

Yesterday, the gloomy fog rolled in. I saw the full moon as I drove home. I couldn't see the river, though the river is only fifty feet through my window sightline. Where there are ordinarily blue skies, today there is a dirty white sky. I woke three times last night and have been doing that the last few nights. I've also had night sweats, which suggests perimenopause. For the last handful of years, my periods have been irregular, yet more frequent. I try to track them, but now my screen notification tells me I'm having my period three times a month.

This morning, I sit with a cup of Earl Grey

Tea, a heavy head and sore muscles. In the last twelve hours, I've had two teenage daughters tell everyone they weren't feeling well either; because they were speaking in a sharp, cutting way, which suggests I'm not the only one nearing my period (I'm wise enough not to ask). Their unkindnesses toward each other sound louder and more intense. I have yet to experience full cramping, yet the nigglings of soreness tell me something is going on down there. I want to cry just to expel the intensity.

I'm a homeschool mama about to have my period. To top it off, today is Tuesday, my busiest homeschool day. It's a regular day of homeschooling, I have writing and homestead projects, and an afternoon and evening driving my children to and from extracurricular activities.

If I'm ill, or feeling PMSy, I can't call anyone to replace me for a sick day. And I'm not the type of mom who wants to watch documentaries or go to the playground if I'm not feeling up to the regular routine. I want to be that mom, but I'm not. I'm the mom who gets down to business no matter how I feel. I hear the arguments start between two kids and I jump in to squash the argument before it gets out of hand. I'm not particularly flexible when I'm being interrupted during work. This present intensity could surely be harnessed to fuel our car for the drive to our afternoon extracurriculars.

Yet I've learned this: I have to honour my womanhood, honour my cycle. Every woman has different manifestations of premenstrual tension. Some women declare they don't have any. Many women experience moodiness, depressive feelings, and/or pain. We're all different: a monthly cycle of how we feel, how we sleep, how we eat, and surely, how we educate.

Observe & plan. Observe your emotions around this time by journaling sleep cycles and emotional needs. Do you identify consistent monthly triggers toward frustration, sadness, or anxiety? Perhaps you're super tired or in pain?

Pay attention to how your family responds to you and how you may be affecting your family. Are you quicker to react to kids' arguing? Are you more sensitive to your partner's inattentiveness? Are you less energetic? Do the kids demand more of your attention or feel less heard?

When I wasn't self-aware and was not paying attention to my cycle, I believed I was my feelings. I didn't identify I was a person having feelings, or that my feelings were my identity.

When I paid attention, I noticed that noise felt overwhelming. On these days, I prefer low energy activities. I want to wrap myself in a blanket, wear my cozy pajamas, munch on salty treats, and hunker down. My goal is to let myself do whatever feels comforting.

I find this hunkering down approach challenging because my kids have the same number of dance classes, part-time jobs, and choir rehearsals to attend. I encounter the same sibling rivalry issues, complaining, and learning challenges (though they feel more frequent during this time). No one sympathizes or asks what they can do for me. My daughters are still learning about their own monthly menstrual needs. And I need to advocate for myself, so they can learn from me.

I need to work to balance my hormones through the use of herbal supplements: vitamin B complex, vitamin D, and magnesium regularly. And possibly other stress supplements, like ashwagandha, cava cava, and L-theanine. I might use aromatherapy, contraceptives, massages, hot baths with Epsom salts, music, wine, or my favourite magazine. I might intentionally increase exercise, sex, dark chocolate, and zinc consumption.

In the local school system, teachers get personal development days. These are days kids don't show up for school; rather, the teachers meet with educational experts and are provided professional development. It's a blue moon in June a homeschool mama gets that kind of day. We might not get PD days, but we can advocate for our PMS days.

Perhaps the kids know when the bag of Lays potato chips and peanut M&Ms arrive, this is the day the family watches documentaries. Consider blocking off a day a month in honour of your cycle. Help a homeschooled kid out, put your cycle on your calendar, and anticipate the day. Identify how your mood shifts, as well as your physical experiences, whether you feel snacky, irritable, foggy, or edgy.

Be kind to yourself. This ain't Groundhog Day. You know you're doing this again next month. Observe your feelings, identify your needs, then plan.

Mama's Pregnancy & Post-Partum

There's nothing like pregnancy or a baby to spice up a homeschool. If you were bored before, you won't be now.

Expect the crazy. You haven't slept in months and are falling asleep reading board books to your toddler while breastfeeding your infant. Your toddler has discovered the cupboard with the open marshmallow bag and is doing her own science experiment: how many marshmallows will clog the toilet?

This is after she found your eyeliner pencil and started her Picasso rendition on the bathroom wall. The baby is still on a two-hour feed schedule twenty-four-seven. He's cute, and good thing, because he only contributes fart smiles and temporary entertainment for the older kids. He's usually lodged in a car seat in the corner of the kitchen, hoping for a little social contact.

The kindergartener is supposed to be reading his new BOB books, but he'd rather play with Lego. He lets you know that as you try to wrangle him on the couch beside your nursing body. You finally give up. When he's not playing with Lego, he's fighting over toys in the playroom with his older sister, who is supposed to be finishing her cursive. He wanted you to listen to the story of his dream this morning, but instead, he's nagging his sister. You text your partner before lunchtime certain there's no way you're going to survive this chaos.

This is the pregnancy and postpartum period. (And I haven't even mentioned the baby's addiction to meals at three in the morning, the other kids' fascination with mama's doughy tummy, or your spontaneous tears at phone commercials.)

Ask for help. Enlist help from grandma or a neighbour, but most certainly enlist help from the one who helped you make this baby. He doesn't know what you need. (I'm still hoping my twenty-year husband will learn to mind read; so far, not looking so good). You'll need to ask him for help, kindly.

Get comfortable with his non-cooking ways as you eat more Campbell's Chunky stews, and bread and butter, but accept the help as you're given it because your cooking and cleaning hours need to decrease so you can sit on the sofa. Kitchen smells are killing you in the first trimester anyway, so it's useful to keep away from the kitchen no matter what you're being served for meals.

Hire help. Now is the time to hire a homeschool kid to be a mother's helper. This was one of the best things I did as a new mom with my third baby. I spent more time leisurely adjusting to sleep deprivation with that babe than I did with even my first baby. All because a gal named Caryn, a teenager, hired to look after our older two girls. I chose to enjoy my girls when I wasn't sleeping with my baby, so I

> Don't keep that routine slavishly; enjoy the routine because it serves you.

gave Caryn the household chore list. (At the end of that summer, I cried when I thanked her because I knew my house would never be that clean again. I was right.)

Keep to the basics. Reading, writing, and arithmetic. If you must add science, think reproductive physiology and bring the kiddos to your doctor's appointments, or think child development and bring them to public health appointments to chat with the health professionals and call this a science field trip. You'll have many of them.

Learn to say no. This isn't the time you should be volunteering to lead a class in the homeschool co-op or caring for other kids in the church nursery.

Add read a-louds to breastfeeding. The benefit of sitting on the sofa with your baby is that your older kiddos will join you. Add educational videos, documentaries, or audiobooks and you'll keep the kids learning.

Keep a daily routine. Don't keep that routine slavishly; enjoy the routine because it serves you. Leave a box of cereal on the counter with bowls and a two liter of milk so when the kids wake up, you can take your coffee to your room, so you can get as many uninterrupted minutes as you can. Then gather them in the kitchen to do their morning studies: read aloud on the sofa, do a math page, cursive page, and recite their poem or do a writing prompt. Then send them to the backyard to play in the sandbox or play yard, so you can sit quietly with the baby on the sofa again. Make a routine that works for you.

Get out of the house. Just anywhere. The park, the grocery store, a museum, or an art gallery. Whatever the kids' attention will allow.

Encourage your kids' independence. This is the time they learn to be independent. Workbooks anyone? This is the period of a homeschool life for which colourful workbooks were designed.

Teach them to take care of you. I didn't say enslave your children, or break out the ylang-ylang, and demand a mama massage. Instead, if they're capable, ask them to bring you a cup of tea, the bottle of ibuprofen, or turn on the aromatherapy diffuser. Sometimes a mama needs a little help from her kids.

Plan, plan, plan. Your plans will get thwarted still, but your plans have a fighting chance. If it's important to you the kids continue with their Latin lessons for the next few months, sit them down with a calendar, then clearly explain the calendar. Let them know what to do and when.

Outline a daily schedule so they know that from 9-12, they're doing their journal entry, reciting their poem three times, writing a half-page of cursive, completing one page of math, and doing a writing assignment for twenty minutes. Or whatever is on your plan.

Be realistic. If your kids haven't done Latin before, this is the wrong time to introduce declensions. If you don't want a stream of questions, do not introduce them to something new or something that requires much explanation.

Give yourself a six-month pass. Let yourself snuggle with the youngest on your bed in the afternoon. Assume you're wearing PJs for six months (then you can transition into the homeschool mama uniform, the yoga pant).

Stop doing studies. Let it go, let it go. If you

can't manage a study routine, then don't. No child will die with six months of no formalized school. You'll come to see your children have learned along the way without formal studies.

Accept the slow mode. There is the slow food movement, and now there are slow studies. This is one of the times in your homeschool when you need to practice being realistic. Yes, you want to do chemistry experiments with your five-year-old. I mean, he is officially in kindergarten now. But girlfriend, you haven't slept through the night for days, weeks, months, or possibly years if this is your second or subsequent child. Go slow mode.

Mama's Perimenopause (& other reasons for natural supplements)

Many changes occur during the menopausal years. Primarily that we women no longer have a period and don't bear children.

Everyone experiences different symptoms. Perimenopause typically lasts around four years. We might experience hot flashes, fatigue, increased premenstrual syndrome, irregular menstrual cycles, insomnia, vaginal dryness, decreased libido, mood swings, anxiety, breast tenderness, and/or moustache growth. (Thank goodness, I'm blond.)

If premenstrual tension affects our homeschools, we can assume a list of perimenopausal symptoms will affect our homeschools too.

Dr. Christiane Northrup, an obstetrician/gynecologist, and author of *Goddesses Never Age* provides perimenopausal advice. Northrup suggests that at around age 42, women go through a midlife crisis where we begin to recognize the timeline of our souls. We ask ourselves, "Really? Is this what I want to do for the rest of my life?" If we ignore the mid-life clarion call for purpose, our stress will increase. Life requires a reset button at this point.

> If we ignore the mid-life clarion call for purpose, our stress will increase. Life requires a reset button at this point.

How stress affects hormones. Some women discover if they eat a lot of sugar, drink a lot of red wine, or are under a lot of stress, they'll get a lot of hot flashes. Stress hormones change the way hormones are metabolized in our bodies.

We have distinct nutritional needs at this time of our lives. When we don't have enough nutrition and necessary supplements, our brains become starved for what they need, and our brains can get depressed. When these things are in place, most people won't need extra hormones.

Estrogen dominance is the gold standard prescription for women who have hot flashes and midnight wakings. Dr. Northrup suggests we need bioidentical hormones; hormones that mimic what our female body already produces. Because we can't patent natural substances, we must create things not found in nature. Many hormones offered by the pharmaceutical industry are not bioidentical. There are so many natural alternatives to bioidentical hormones.

> Remember to consult your physician or natural health practitioner before following the advice in this chapter.

Do all women need bioidentical hormones? Dr. Northrup suggests substances and supplements should be considered carefully, especially when one is taking any medications, or being overseen by a medical practitioner.

I was trained as a Registered Nurse in the western medicine model, and I've been married to a medical physician who has worked in the western medicine for twenty years. Naturopathic or eastern medical approaches are not my training; however, I live in a community that encourages wholistic health care and my health has been reaping the benefits, so I can't NOT share naturopathic and eastern medicine possibilities with you:

➢ **Taurine**, an amino sulfonic acid, is a building block of protein, and has been used for perimenopause. Taurine is known to improve attention, memory, and reasoning. (All necessary characteristics for a homeschool mama).

➢ **Passionflower** is useful in easing middle of the night wakings, decreasing anxiety, helping to regulate mood, and regulating sleep-wake cycles. Passionflower enables deeper sleep and relaxation.

➢ **Turmeric** comes from the root of a flowering plant of the ginger family. Turmeric's active compound, curcumin, has shown to improve major depression, promote resilience to stress, and reduce anxiety.

➢ **St. John's Wort** is an herb that helps the brain increase uptake of serotonin, dopamine and norepinephrine. It can relieve anxiety. Sometimes St. John's Wort is as effective as an SSRI (an antidepressant), so if you're taking an SSRI, consult your physician.

➢ **Theanine**, when taken with caffeine, is known to enable people to switch between tasks more fluidly. (Ummm, where have you been all my parenting life?) If taken each night for eight weeks, theanine can decrease depression too.

➢ **5-HTP** helps with sleep and depression and is a chemical byproduct of tryptophan, increasing the brain hormone serotonin. (Or you could just consume a turkey every day; lots of tryptophan in that too).

➢ **Black Cohosh is used to reduce hot flashes, excessive sweating, and night sweats.**

➢ **Get your Vitamin D to optimum levels.** Women who have optimal levels of Vitamin D reduce their breast cancer risk by 80%. (Having a few babies will also help decrease breast cancer, if you're open to that. I'm not, ha.)

➢ **Get enough iodine.** You can get these through kelp, seaweed, or Lugol solution.
➢ **Get enough magnesium. This m**ight be why some women crave dark chocolate. Magnesium helps you get a good night sleep and helps treat hormonal imbalance.

> ➢ **Get your Omega 3 supplements. Or regularly consume f**laxseed oil or a bi-weekly consumption of Coldwater fish.

Change your diet by consuming garden herbs, making healthier food choices, and decreasing caffeine consumption.

Use adaptogens. These herbs are used to decrease symptoms of stress, including forgetfulness, exhaustion, and sleep issues.

> ➢ **Rhodiola** is known to reduce anxiety, fatigue, and depression. Rhodiola is an adaptogenic herb that assists the adrenals by reducing stress-related fatigue.

> ➢ **Ashwagandha and holy basil are** adaptogens that help our body manage stress, correct imbalances in the neuroendocrine, and immune systems. It significantly reduces anxiety and stress.

> ➢ **Asian ginseng** is an adaptogen that supports cognitive function and reduces mental fatigue, boosts mental alertness, low energy, and improves memory.

Use natural substances found in your garden *(or your friend who sells essential oils, because we all have at least one):*

> ➤ **Lemon Balm** is a lemon-scented herb that generates sedative effects, is antiviral, and has digestive health benefits. Lemon balm grows easily in a garden and makes a delicious tea.

> ➤ **Chamomile** is an extract from German chamomile flowers. It is used to improve sleep quality and decrease nighttime awakenings. It may help with menstrual period pain as well. It makes a tea too, but not so delicious.

Aromatherapy & essential oils. Essential oils are the Tupperware of the 2010s. Clary sage contains phytoestrogens and is known to regulate the menstrual cycle by balancing hormone levels naturally. Lavender is popular for a reason: it smells good. Lavender also helps improve symptoms of depression, insomnia, and chronic fatigue. (There are many essential oil options — just ask your friend.)

These regular activities will help you during perimenopause:
> ➤ **Exercise.** A half-hour a day minimum that burns off that tension, girlfriend. Increase serotonin in your brain, which also wards off depression.

➢ **Deep breathing exercises, meditation, and yoga are life-changers, if you haven't tried them already**. Anything to decrease that extra blast of anxiety you gain as a perimenopausal woman. (Have I sold you on meditation and yoga already?)

➢ **Acupuncture** is known to increase estrogen levels, decrease levels of FSH and LH, increase estrogen receptor protein expression inhibiting GnRH, and transform androgen into estrogen.[1] And in my personal experience, it just feels good.

➢ **Functional medicine and Chinese medicine consultations**. Perimenopausal symptoms originate from unique hormonal imbalances for individual women so these specialists can help manage your unique needs.

Accept western medicine too. If I was in a car accident, I wouldn't head to my naturopath, I'd go to Emerg like everyone else in the western world. If I wanted to enable my overall well-being, I'd head to my alternative health practitioner, not the medical world. There's a lot of present-day development in the science around women's health. Other options to research:

➢ **Femarone 17,** a natural progesterone supplement, helps with sleep.

➢ Testosterone pellets or creams.

➢ Heart math.

➢ Bio-Identical Hormones.

And now for the kids: just as you let the kids know you're premenstrual, let them know you're experiencing the challenges of perimenopause. Kids deserve to be forewarned.

Mama's Sexuality

This won't be a manual on how to have sex. I know you know how to do it. It's why you're homeschooling. Can't have homeschooling without sex. (Actually, there's adoption, artificial insemination, and foster care, but they're not helping me make my point.)

Sexual intimacy might be a challenge when you have kids in your home most all the time that you're also in the house. Laundry rooms with sliding doors are unwise options, so personal experience has taught me. In front of the giant Italian fireplace on the luxurious bear rug in a vacation rental is a lifetime happy memory for me and my partner, not so much for our nine-year-old.

"Why can't I open the bedroom door? It's locked. Mom, Mom, I need you. Jessie took my Barbie." Great timing, again.

"I'll be right out," we answer in our mama voice. You stop in suspended animation inside the walls of your bedroom. How do you be an engaged partner and be a homeschool mom?

Just as you can Christmas shop while young kids are with you, you can find a way to have sex when they're little. Distraction, distraction, distraction. (Though you

> How do you be an engaged partner and be a homeschool mom?

and your partner won't fit into a coat-covered shopping cart, you can find a way.)

Once your children enter the prepubescent age, they begin to ask questions. Their sexuality questions begin with, "Where did my little brother come from?" When they can have open conversations with their parents, they come to understand their siblings were born in a moment of passion between their parents. *Ewww.*

We all know that kids will eventually understand that their parents are sexually active more than the number of times their siblings were born. When adolescence arrives, we'll have more complex challenges than discussions. We will surely be challenged to find a nondescript place to be discrete. When kids enter adolescence, they know when you're sneaking a gift for them into the cart, and they know when you're sneaking yourselves into your locked bedroom.

Once those teenagers get to bed later than you, quiet moments are difficult to find. Sex doesn't have to be in your home. A love shack in the forest? A weekly rendezvous at a cheap motel? Behind a locked door at his office? Tent time in the backyard? A weekend away with kids at the grandparents? Trade weekends with other friends who have kids.

In the magical teenage years, an ear for deep breathing, locked doors, and disappearing parents makes them awfully curious. There's no getting around their growing awareness. Give your children fair warning: if the door is closed, they can decide if they want PTSD. So many choices in adolescence.

Benefits of sexual regularity: endorphins are released that increase our happy energy. The oxytocin hormone released post-orgasm, the same hormone we experience after giving birth is also the hormone that makes us feel connected to our partner and our baby. Oxytocin makes us want to connect and feel attached to our partner. When we have a partner to be attached to, the unity and connection created helps us take on all the random, unexpected, hearty challenges we homeschool mamas face.

How often? Just fifteen minutes every day, fifteen times a week. Just kidding. Whatever works for the two of you.

When to do it? At the end of a long day, after meals are made, the house is tidied, the laundry is folded, games are played, read alouds are read, French grammar is studied, Latin prayers are recited, and passages are dictated, then sex is on the schedule. (Insert laugh track here).

Sex can seem like just one more thing to do. One more thing you don't have to do. Even if, in theory, you want to do it. Your relationship thrives with sex. Enjoy it as much as you enjoy a bag of Lays potato chips. Relish it as much as you relish an uninterrupted morning coffee. *Whatever you do, make sure sex is bullet-pointed on your weekly Day Timer. Just fifteen minutes, ha.*

Mama Does the Homeschool Hygge

Homeschool hygge: these two words go together like apple and pie, Italy and pizza, fireplace and book, beach and margarita.

Nothing like a cold day to entice us to the

sofa with a few cozy blankets and our read-alouds or workbooks. Light the warm, burnt orange candles, start a fire in the fireplace, and turn on Spotify to a classical composer like Pelecis.

The first day of frost arrived last week. The puppy's water froze. The chickens hesitated to leave the coop. I hesitated to walk the puppy under the almost touchable morning cloud cover. Snow flurries were forecast for the morning and the blue sky was white by lunchtime. The kids found their winter gear and were outside building a snow companion dog for our puppy. They also made a couple snow forts and their first sledding trail.

> Seasonal and hormonal shifts are the big yellow triangular signs that tell us to slow down and do the homeschool hygge.

The seasonal shifts draw us to hygge, just as our monthly hormonal changes do as well. Seasonal and hormonal shifts are the big yellow triangular signs that tell us to slow down and do the homeschool hygge.

Hygge is defined by the Merriam-Webster Dictionary as a quality of coziness that makes a person feel content and comfortable.

Hygge is all about being in the moment, feeling completely relaxed, letting go of the hectic world around you, either alone or with loved ones. No phones and computers allowed in those magical moments.

My top twenty happy homeschool hygge practices:

- ➢ **Kitty cats.** Even if it's a hamster, cuddly furry things help kids focus. Kitties in the kids' bedrooms with math is a happy homeschool hygge practice.

- ➢ **Tea. A** common homeschool beverage. In the fall and winter, it is a must. Unless it's morning, then drink coffee. (My kids would add cookies too.)

- ➢ **Candles,** lots and lots of candles. Candles are just cozy.

- ➢ **Fireplaces blazing.** Nothing says cozy like a warming fire, workbooks, textbooks, pencils, and erasers in front of the fireplace.

- ➢ **Pajamas.** Does it need to be said that pajamas scream homeschool hygge? What homeschool family isn't already using this practice?
- ➢ **Morning skincare routine.** Perhaps you've been doing this for a coon's age. I'm shamefully, relatively new to this skincare thing. Just in time for my 45th birthday.

(Good thing I have teenage girls to teach me.)

➢ **Chocolate and wine.** Two ounces of dark chocolate after dinner. Wine for weekends. These practices are decadent homeschool mama luxuries. I think we should have a homeschool mama wine club too. Anyone in?

➢ **Morning cuddles with books and blankies.** Afternoon cuddles with books and blankies. Evening cuddles with books, teddies and cute kids. Yeah, so the trend: lots of cuddles, lots of blankies, and lots of books. (And yes, mama needs a blankie too).

➢ **Neighbourhood walks.** In the autumn morning frost or in the golden afternoon sun, outdoor walks are nature therapy. We more gratefully return inside and start a fire, grab a book, a cup of tea, and sit to read.

➢ **Afternoon skis on the canal in winter flurries.** Living in a picture-perfect moment, breathing in the great outdoors, we notice nature and observe its ever-changing process when we're in it daily.

➢ **Documentaries.** Watching documentaries in the afternoon. Curiosity Stream, Knowledge Network and CBC are our present favourites.

➢ **Hot food.** Freshly baked bread and savoury soup for lunch.

➢ **Fast food.** Crockpot or InstaPot creations warming on the counter make dinner plans less complicated. No McDonald's drive-thru required.

➢ **Spotify** warming the sound waves. We build our own classical playlists for morning studies, movie soundtrack playlists for afternoon reading, and Top 20 Friday night dance party songs.

➢ A hot tub dip at the end of the day. This hygge moment is brought to you by future aspirations: because we don't have a wood burning hot tub yet, I'll also take a hot bath.

➢ **Sleeping in**. Sleep sufficiency is a total advantage to homeschooling. I am not a master of sleeping in. Unless you think 7 am is sleeping in, but we can give our children the sleeping-in freedom when the days are dark and dreary.

- ➤ **Hot beverages. Yerba mate,** coffee, hot chocolate, or chai tea belong to every season, every single morning. Pumpkin spice lattes for fall. Peppermint chocolate for winter. Two cappuccinos on dreary days. A cappuccino with toast and homemade apricot jam in the garden on summer days.

- ➤ **Choose your schedule.** Finish writing and math studies by lunch. And read, read, read the afternoon away.

- ➤ **Choose one subject a week** and enjoy that subject thoroughly.

- ➤ **Delete a subject.** Or write each subject on a slip of paper, throw the subjects in a jar, and let the kids pick one out to omit that week. Definitely homeschool hygge for the kids.

CARING FOR MAMA'S MIND

"It takes courage to grow up and Become who you really are."
-EE Cummings

Become You.
 If you don't know who you are, you don't know what you need.

Something happens when one takes on the role of mama. Mama becomes nurturer, guide, and teacher. Since there isn't a moment in the day she isn't mama, she can get consumed by that role and forget she has a non-mama identity.

Recognize yourself as a separate person with unique needs. "You be You," the cool folks say. But who be you?

Women develop and grow as we mature in our motherhood. But you don't have to let go of who you were before you were a mother.

Before I was a mother, I was a newly trained registered nurse with adventurous hopes in becoming a nurse practitioner in the Arctic and Africa. I liked watching movies, perusing bookstores with tall lattes, writing stories, compiling scrapbooks, and timidly engaged in social scenarios. What occupied your spare time before you had a family? What activities did you love?

How would you describe yourself? **Take stock of your general character and personality.** I am a homeschool mama of four kids. I am organized, empathic, no-nonsense, impatient, spontaneous, fun, methodical, intentional, and occasionally perseverating. I am a philosopher and a natural-born encourager. Meyers Briggs defines me as an ENFJ and Enneagram tells me I am a type 3, with a wing of 7. I can talk to anyone, yet I tire of small talk. I like to share what I know, but I'm not a teacher. I'm a planner, an idea creator, a creative, but not in the sewing, watercolour art way. I like keeping an annual reading goal. I designed two homes, designed a chicken coop and researched raising chickens. I've raised a large guardian puppy. I have written four books, and marketed this book.

Who are you? Have you explored your personality through Meyers Briggs or Enneagram profiling? (You can do a quick on-line quiz and learn more about yourself.) What activities do you enjoy? What curiosities do you have?

Just as important as acknowledging our interests and personality is acknowledging our emotional inner world. *Pay attention to your internal emotional landscape.* How do you react, feel, or think? Different scenarios likely create different internal experiences for you. What makes you feel angry, disappointed, cheerful, sad, delighted? Do you consciously know what thoughts preoccupy you and why? How do you engage those feelings when you have them?

Sit and listen. Self-awareness helps us attend to ourselves and makes us more aware of how we can attend to others too. Over time, when we repeatedly listen to our internal world, we know who we are and what we're about, and we know what we're not. We become familiar with our internal thought and emotional landscape. We know how we react; we learn to respond, not react, to those emotional triggers.

We recognize that when more than one child talks, we feel overwhelmed. We recognize that when more than one child is complaining, we feel irritated.

Reading a book with a glass of wine makes a perfect Friday night. We don't care that our interests lie in finishing our Goodreads reading list and it might be boring to some. We know what interests we want to occupy our time.

> Not everyone is interested in us becoming our own person. Others might have a different prescription for us.

Over time, we learn who we are in relation to what others expect of us. Instead of trying to be what we believe others expect of us, we let loose and be. We don't care that others expect us to be sophisticated when we're simple, expect us to enjoy ladies' brunch when we'd rather be at home in our jammies, or expect us to invest our time researching climate change when we'd rather watch reality tv. We don't care that others downhill ski in the winter months and that our family might be the only family in town that doesn't. We can be us without requiring others' approval.

Not everyone is interested in us becoming our own person. Others might have a different prescription for us. Becoming more you might mean you may no longer fill the same role in their world. Maybe you're the one that lets anyone talk, spew their stories till there is no more story. Maybe you're the one that rescues them from their struggle. They'll benefit from you becoming more you, so they can stand on their own two feet.

So, keep learning, keep paying attention, keep growing.

If we are self-nurturing and self-affirming, we learn to listen closely to ourselves, what we need, who we are, and what we're all about.

We'll develop such a strong sense of ourselves that we will listen to others' perspectives with respect, honour their feelings when they don't intuitively make sense to us, acknowledge their ways of doing things as merely different, not bad, and honour their needs too. We'll become people who are comfortable being ourselves but also comfortable with others being themselves too.

If you need a refresher to remember who you are, here are a few steps to becoming you:

- ➤ Acknowledge what you liked to do before you were a mother. Do you want to adopt a few of those things in the present?

- ➤ Acknowledge what new aspects of you that you enjoy now. What activities have been added in your life?

- ➤ Identify your emotional challenges.

- ➤ Consider your emotional landscape.

- ➤ In the middle of the night, what wakes you?

- ➤ Make something. Peruse Pinterest, a magazine, or YouTube. What would you want to make if you had all the time in the world or had someone teaching you?

- ➤ Do something you loved to do when you were a child.

- ➤ Recall musical interests you had back in the day. What kind of music concert would you attend if you had the money or time? Book tickets.

➤ Sit with Spotify and a favourite drink and listen to a taped concert, the whole thing. Music is the soundtrack to our lives.

➤ Write a list of the people you value and why.

➤ Write your three most important values, and why they are essential to you. Recognize how they impact your choices.

➤ Find your mantra. For a while, mine was carpe diem. Now that I've seized enough days, I'm seizing other mantras, like, "This life is for learning, for authentically sharing, and being."

➤ Choose your daily words. Write them in your journal each morning. I have four this year: Encourage. Empower. Expand. Invite. These are daily reinforcements that help me focus my intentions on my business, my relationships, and my family.

➤ Spend a day away from the kids. Don't do anything for the family. Then you'll see what interests you. Have no expectations for the day.

➢ Meditate. Every day. Meditation helps us to listen to our inner voice and gives us time to listen to what's going on inside us. When you are still, you hear yourself more.

➢ **We are helping our children become themselves. We**'ve got eighteen years to facilitate their self-learning journey. We facilitate our children's interests and curiosities. However, the self-learning journey is for a lifetime, both for them and for us. We've got us to explore for our entire lives.

"You don't become what you want, you become what you believe."
Oprah Winfrey

Mama's Alone Time

Call it building perspective, call it finding freedom, call it zoning out — whatever you want to call it, you need to have separate time from your kids.

If you have young children, you likely can't fathom there will come a time they don't knock on your door every ten minutes or decide they will be permanently attached to your hip. The time will come when you find they are happily occupied watching cartoons for half an hour, then playing chutes and ladders all afternoon with their siblings. There will come a time when they are not enthused to be part of family read-alouds. There will even come a time when they prefer listening to music in their bedroom or making posters for their wall and would rather not come for family dinner.

When that time comes, we begin to get a glimpse that our parenting journey might come to an end. As we're often told, the days are long, but the years are short.

We homeschool mamas have the privilege of parenting our children most of their young lives, influencing their perspective on the experiences they have inside and outside our homes. We have the privilege of watching them learn to read, develop their math literacy, tackle a new skill, discover a new passion, and we get to guide them in their interpersonal struggles.

> ...whatever you want to call it, you need to have separate time from your kids.

We are blessed. We get to do the very thing we wanted when we became parent. We get to be with our children. Being with our children can take a lot from us. Because we are emotionally invested in our kids, like no one else, we follow them on their emotional roller coasters. We worry about them, pray for them, and search for guidance with them.

With all our emotional investment, attention to detail, and responsibility to emotionally guide, we sometimes find ourselves lost in the mama role, unsure we even exist.

Where did mama go? You're still there, under the mama role somewhere. Continue to explore you as you have time alone.

Your alone time shouldn't include grocery shopping. Don't cheat. I know grocery shopping seems pleasant when you've been homeschooling long enough or have more kids under five than fingers on your hand. If you're thinking grocery shopping is your alone time, this is your sign you need more alone time. Enough time to think two thoughts consecutively, without interruption.

Time alone at home is my favourite. This doesn't happen very often, but I enjoy quiet time at home as much as I enjoy my daughter's chocolate mousse cake. When I get time alone, I usually begin with an exciting clean-up time, sweeping all the floors, wiping counters, and folding laundry. Then I let myself free flow my time, which usually includes

Have a nap for the rest of the moms who wish they could...

reading, writing, and outdoor time (the same things I do with the kids in the house, but quieter).

Time alone in meditation is time well-spent. If you can sit still for fifteen minutes, listen to your breath, try not to think thoughts at all, all the better. Some people call this meditation, others call this a nap. Both will benefit your brain.

Take a nap. Just ten to twenty minutes a day will help reduce your sleep debt and give you increased vigor. If your kids are little and napping, lucky you. Take a nap while you can. Have a nap for the rest of the moms who wish they could or do it because you're about to enter a decade long sleep deficit. If you have two kids, with only one child napping, try to occupy your oldest with books or toys on his bed. If you get to nap, don't lay down with your screen. No screens allowed, unless you're turning on a YouTube meditation to nap.

Use screen time intentionally. Compartmentalize your screen time, so screen time doesn't rule you. We all know it's not healthy to check Facebook notifications every ten minutes but it's easy to do. There is a time and a place to use that screen: you need your device to check appointments, balance the chequing account, or message your mom about where to meet the kids. Screens are useful tools, and they can be fun too, but they can also be potential trouble. They are not useful if they encourage procrastination or if they help you avoid dealing with challenging emotions. You have reasons to use your screens, just use them intentionally.

Exchange your kids for an afternoon a week. Bring your friend's kids to your house for two hours and entertain them with a kiddy pool and a hose; then next week, send your kids to that friend's house, while you have two hours of respite.

If you could spend just fifteen minutes a day, what would you do?

> ➤ Learn to make handmade soap?
> ➤ Learn to arrange flowers?
> ➤ Take piano lessons?
> ➤ Tinker on old piano songs you learned as a child?
> ➤ Meditate with an adult colouring book?
> ➤ Sip on coffee while tapping on Pinterest uninterrupted?
> ➤ Write a book?
> ➤ Start an Etsy shop?

It might take work in the beginning to establish fifteen separate minutes. The kids will learn you are not fooling around when you become consistent and instill boundaries around that time. You really do want separate time, albeit a very short separate time at first. It will be a challenge for the kids to learn those boundaries, and a challenge for you to teach the kids about those boundaries, but you can do it!

➢ For smaller children, a friend or partner might be required to assist.

➢ Can you create a routine of fifteen minutes?

➢ Can you take yourself, your drawing book, pencils, and a journal to a café one evening a week?

➢ Can you carve out fifteen minutes before you leave your bedroom? As I've said before, if your kids are very young, they might need an in-room alarm clock set to ring when they may leave their rooms in the morning. For older kids, have cereal and milk waiting on the kitchen counter.

Just like trying to munch just one kettle chip, you'll want to take another. Gradually those fifteen minutes will grow into more minutes.

Mama Having Fun

Do you remember what you liked to do for fun before the kids arrived?

You might have to go into a twelve-step

program for homeschool mamas if you answer: "I like to make homemade volcanoes, craft human cell candy creations, perform Barbie weddings, and play Roblox."

I know you like hanging with your kids. Of course, you do, that's why you continue to homeschool. You're also a separate person that has unique interests that may or may not be shared with your kids.

"Hi, my name is Teresa. I used to think quiet time meant peeing without interruption and walking the aisles of the grocery store alone. Now I've reclaimed myself: I like to read, write, listen to jazz, drink wine, dance, and watch movies. In the summer I hike, garden and canoe, and meet guests at my bed & breakfast. During winter, I cross country ski, snowshoe, and photograph my chickens, puppy, and homestead."

What do you like to do? Who are you apart from your kids?

Have feel-good moments with the family too. Too often, we homeschoolers like to organize academics, field trips, meal plans, household duties, and chore lists. We drive kids to activities, plan for summer camps, spring break camps, and summer activities, yet we don't expect to let our hair down and have fun with our kids.

Have fun, not because we want to be fun for the kids but because sometimes, we just need to let our hair down, not plan or strategize and do something fun for the sake of fun.

Have regular time with friends. Can you make time in your weekly routine? Even if you're an introvert. If you must, find some introverted friends and sit in a café and pretend to read together while listening to other people have extroverted conversations. If you want to do that without cost, sit in a library and do the same. Better yet, choose one activity you love, like writing poetry, then find a local poetry slam and attend until you connect with someone. Create consistent times with other people you really like, and spend regular time with them.

> I used to think quiet time meant peeing without interruption and walking the aisles of the grocery store alone.

Whatever you do, maintain regularity. Given enough time and consistency, you will surely find reliable, supportive friendships in a social network. Put in the effort and reap the benefit.

Spin the boring stuff. You know the stuff you

do every day? Like every single day? Laundering clothes, washing dishes, vacuuming the floor, sweeping the kitchen, making beds, driving kids to rugby practice, you fill in the blank (I know there's more on this list). Find a way to do them with joy.

There was an afternoon I was super annoyed, okay, maybe even grumbling. I complained to my husband I had to sweep and wash the floor. I was loud enough that everyone in the house knew. My husband tried to diffuse my annoyance (he was living dangerously as I was also premenstrual). He asked me if I had to sweep the floor. "Yes! I have to! Who else is going to do it?" Then he added, "If sweeping is an activity you feel needs to get done, why don't you choose to sweep with joy?" Harumph. I turned on my heels but kept sweeping as he left the room. I took a deep breath and told myself, he's right, it's about time I enjoy the process.

How to redeem the boring stuff, like floor cleaning, driving, or dishwashing? Podcasts, so many podcasts with so many themes. They enrich our lives while we learn from others. Or music exploration time or keeping old tunes alive.

I would be remiss not to add: consider assigning chores to kids. Too young, you say. Is there a too young, really? If they can't balance on two legs, they're too young. If they can balance on two legs, they're never too young to do chores.

Cook with alcohol. No, I don't mean to cook off the alcohol. I don't want to encourage an actual twelve step program, so take this section with a grain of salt. Pretend you're hosting a cooking show. You are indeed cooking every single night. (Unless you've taught the kids to cook, in which case, you deserve an award, like a bottle of wine in a hot tub with the hubby. Can they just bring you a plate to the hot tub?) Otherwise, have fun with the cooking hour once or twice a week with a glass of wine or a margarita.

Listen to your choice of music in the car. We all know a few CDs we turn on in the car to continue our kids' education. Whether this is a geography CD, a Jim Weiss narration, French CD, a musical composer CD, Story of the World series, or an Audible family selection, we homeschoolers often choose to redeem travel time for our kids' education. Sometimes we need to let travel time be downtime. Let the kids learn preferred musical selections and explain the life stories we have tied to those songs. Or learn the coolest songs on the Top Ten. Sing loud, sing along, and have fun.

Schedule coffee with yourself. Twice a day. Once in the morning to wake up. The second coffee can be enjoyed after lunch, with a tiny little cookie that only you consume (and don't let the kids know they exist. I plant mine under the corner chair in my master bedroom; don't tell my kids). I close the door, pull out the iPad, and tap on Pinterest for a few minutes: homeschooling, gardening, homesteading, writing ideas, or random stuff I'll possibly never use but imagine I might one day.

Head to a cafe once a week. And if you must include the kids, bring the kids with a book or a game. Let them spend their own allowance money on a strawberry Frappuccino and let them get to work. Bring a magazine to read or as a foil. Stick your screen in the folded pages and tap on Hay Day. Kids don't have to be the only ones who sneak screens.

Add novelty. Do something different. The day in day out nature of homeschooling can be dulling at times. Especially when the days get shorter, and inside time gets longer. What can you do that might be different from your typical routine? A field trip to somewhere that has long been on your to-do list? A trip to an indoor skating rink? Change the order of studies. Try laser tag or paint ball. Try a different sport or a different library in a new town.

Consider the seasons. I don't know what it is like to live without seasons. I take the climatic seasons as a sign to shake things up a bit. Fun Fridays are infused with activities like hiking, basketball, biking, tennis, and skiing. Can't cross country ski in the summer. Can't bike in four feet of snow. Take advantage of the seasons if you've got them.

Whatever you do, find your fun.

Mama Keeps Learning

There are only so many mornings you can show someone how to write a cursive uppercase H, or teach another kiddo how to do long division, or memorize prepositions through poetry. Eventually you'll wonder if you also could pursue your interests. Yes, yes, you can!

Your curiosity helps everyone dive deeper into study. Your interest is infectious and facilitates your children's curiosity also. If you love to learn, they will too.

Every bit of education makes an interesting, engaged human. Your homeschool will naturally evolve and shift just like your interests and curiosities evolve and shift over the years. When you pay attention to the learning needs and interests of your children and yourself, your home education becomes dynamic. When you include you in your home education, you create a family version of an education.

Your mental stimulation matters. Those sweet little voices surrounding you every day compel you to engage all sorts of subjects you hadn't imagined. I've had an opportunity to study geology, British history, and American politics. They aren't my first choice, but they've expanded my

> Your interest is infectious and facilitates your children's curiosity also.

mind. Legos, Barbies, and Wild Kratts dominated our calendar in the early years, and they weren't so expansive — despite being asked by sweet little voices. Those sweet little voices will be saying, "I love you" at the airport as they fly off to discover a different part of the world, learning about themselves somewhere else.

What do your kids see you learning? My kids have watched me write in cafes (where I've asked them to sit quietly with a book or play cards beside me, and I have learned to compartmentalize mentally). They have watched me build garden beds one rock at a time, draft and build a house (with an architect and a bunch of talented builders, not with my own two hands), watched me learn to care for chickens, and train a large guardian puppy, and build a homestead and start a bed and breakfast.

Consider how you like to learn. You know who wants to study elephants, who likes mixing concoctions on the kitchen counter, who likes squirreling themselves into their bedrooms, or reading the afternoon away. How do you like to learn?

➢ Are you an avid podcast listener?

➢ Do you watch educational YouTubes when the kids are napping?

➢ Do you have regular subscriptions to specialty magazines?

➢ Do you like to experiment in the kitchen?

➢ Do you like listening to Zoom casts or Facebook lives?

➢ Would you rather listen to an instructor in a classroom with twenty other students and engage with them?

➢ Or would you rather settle into your room with a few books, a candle, and a do not disturb sign outside your door (P.S. don't buy that sign, it might work with a hotel housemaid, but it won't work with your kids).

Dabble in your interests. My kids know I'm fond of art history, classical music, literature, poetry, and new languages. We include my interests in our homeschool days because I like them, and I want to share those interests with them.

Just because we're curious about what atomic theory means doesn't mean we have to become an atomic theorist. Just because our kids are interested in the Chem C500 experiment box when they're eleven, doesn't mean they're going to be chemists. Dabble in your interests, just like you encourage them to dabble in theirs.

You don't need to commit to an ETSY shop in hand lettering. You don't have to purchase a water colour set if you're just curious. You don't need to be committed to hand lettering, crocheting, goat herding, culinary blogging, or decoupaging. No commitment necessary. Just dabble.

Your education reminds you that you are separate. If you are interested in any aspect of history, include your interest. If you like any element of science, include your interest. You love writing? Reading? Critiquing? Debating? Tinkering? Creating? You know what I'm going to say: include your interest.

What are the things you want to learn? Play in your learning. This is the most effective form of learning for our kids, so this approach will work for us too. If you don't already have a pressing interest you wish to expand, get yourself a Pinterest account and pin until an interest appears. Coursera and Khan Academy are available for adults, too, not just homeschooled teenagers.

Pursue formal education. College classes and community classes abound. Who says you can't take classes alongside your kiddos? Yes, that might mean you need to change your homeschool routine, you might need to approach the kids' studies differently; you might need to change. Maybe you need to consider unschooling your children for a season, hire tutors, or send them to school if you need a season of your own formal education. This is a gigantic commitment but homeschool will await you when you return if you decide this education is important to you.

Sign up for Learning. Sign up for interesting email newsletters, TedX accounts, and magazine subscriptions. And if you do this, plan a time in the week when you'll do these activities.

Learn about learning. You might not need to learn to manage a classroom of twenty-five, you probably won't find a use for educationese, but learning about learning will help your kids, and your patience, if you learn more about how your kids learn.

Play but don't expect great things. You might discover that a drawing class is a fabulous idea but requires more mental effort than you could have imagined when you stood in that class with your easel, graphite pencils, and squishy eraser. Estimating the size and angle of that vase seemed like a simple thing when watching Bob Ross. Now you know you officially are no Picasso. You don't want to do this anymore. Then don't. Remember, you're playing, so play.

Spend three minutes after lunch when the kids are cleaning the kitchen, and you're sitting with a cup of coffee and an Italian cookie in a quiet room and peruse those books. Maybe you'll never borrow a book on Michelangelo's sculptures again. Perhaps you'll spend months learning why he was enlisted to paint the Sistine chapel when his real love was sculpting. Maybe you'll even plan your trip to Florence.

Invest just 15 minutes. Fifteen minutes is easily overspent on Facebook or chatting on the phone. Tell the kids you're unavailable for those fifteen minutes, or enlist a partner, a neighbour or a friend to enforce that fifteen minutes and focus your attention on that curiosity. Fifteen minutes will gradually expand into an hour a day, maybe three hours a day, when your kids are older.

Caveat though: **limit screen time.** I'm not calling you out, mama. Use your screen any way you want. If you're like many, screen time is not a free-for-all in your home. The kids know the screen will time out, or they can only have screens after dinner or in the morning for a short burst. Yet you have access to screens whenever you desire. I know you often use that screen to organize your life, message someone about a playdate, check that email telling you where you need to be this afternoon, or search a question your kiddo asked earlier. And yet, we all know how easy it is to get lost in that device. I check on Facebook marketplace if someone bought my dining room light, and I find myself trying to figure out if my friend is really in a South African airport right now, because my sister just flew through Johannesburg yesterday. I'm lost somewhere over Africa when I could be fully engaged with my child right now.

> I'm lost somewhere over Africa when I could be fully engaged with my child right now.

Your education is as important as your kiddos. Yes, I know, you got an education once upon a time. Your longest-lasting, most memorable explorations are often self-directed, self-taught. So be inspired and pursue your own learning.

Read with intention. If you're not a proficient reader, time to pick up the pursuit. When you bring your kids to the library each week, because that's also a common homeschool habit, let them peruse their children's or teen section while you wander over to any other section and explore the great unknown. Borrow as many books as your card allows, a book for each day perhaps.

> Your longest-lasting, most memorable explorations are often self-directed, self-taught.

Mama's Self-Care Activity a Day Plan

If you're not in the practice of doing something fun or self-nurturing every day, plan just one activity a day. Just like you schedule exercise each day and meals three times a day, plan a fun activity every day. Even if it's only fifteen minutes.

Manicure Monday. Monday's a busy day so

keep your self-care activity simple. When Monday evening hits and I'm melting into the couch, I give myself a manicure.

Taco Tuesdays with my daughter at the local Cantina and a coconut habanero half-margarita is my favourite Tuesday self-care strategy. The energy is lively, entirely different than the energy of my child-based world. Except that I'm with one of my kids, who is still underage, so no margarita for her.

Wednesday is girls' night out. Go to a movie, go out for a drink, meet for coffee, or text message a friend. Nurture your social circle.

Thursday is online gaming night with my son. I'm not into online gaming, though I did have that Hay Day game phase where I swiped eggs from chicken coops. Now that I have a real chicken coop, Cluckingham Palace, with fifteen princesses and King Henry the 8th, I gather real eggs. Now I know I have to wipe those eggs, not swipe those eggs. Thursday could also be a Reading Night with the girls. If I can fit a chapter in a week, twice a week even better, with my teenage girls, I'm having fun. Sense and Sensibility with one, and something purely fun and silly with the younger because she would fall asleep faster than I could finish the first line to any Jane Austen novel.

Fun Friday: Friday morning we play a jeopardy-style game quizzing Canadian History, World Geography, Governments, or French terminology (or whatever they're studying). Then Professor Noggins games, Bananagrams, Boggle, math dice games, Curiosity Stream, or documentaries. After that we head outdoors to ski and sit in a cabin with a mug of hot chocolate and muffins. If it's spring or fall, we find a hiking trail to wander. Friday night is wine and film night. A nice glass of something velvety, round, plummy on the nose, and black pepper on the tongue. Oh, and an Academy Award-nominated film. Or something funny with Melissa McCarthy. Or an old black and white film.

I use my **Saturday technology morning** eagerly, because I wait till then to get around to all those email newsletters to which I've subscribed, and I tour my Twitter account, and Facebook feed. Saturday, I insert snippets of reading throughout my homeschool days. Still Saturday night I include more challenging reading, like short stories by Alice Munro, Wuthering Heights by Charlotte Bronte, and passages from Ernest Hemmingway. I like to read an evening away, with less challenging stuff too: like women's travel anthology, memoirs by Trevor Noah or Mindy Kaling or a clever book-turned-film like The Time Traveler's Wife. I make Goodreads goals to finish a certain number of books every year — my kind of fun.

Saturday night can also be date night. We don't have to spend a fortune for date night, but if we have a partner, we do have to have separate time with just that partner, no kids. Costco sampling stations for two? Dollar store discovery? Motel Six surprise visits? Something fun, something novel, but only the two of you.

> Despite the close-knit family lifestyle, when the kids get bigger, there's less time together.

On Sunday, I like an afternoon out, to an art gallery, a hike with a picnic, or a canoe trip. If I lived in New York City, I would head to the Met every Sunday. Alas, I do not. Though I do peruse our local galleries regularly. Sunday night can be **family games night.** Despite the close-knit family lifestyle, when the kids get bigger, there's less time together. There are more friends, more part-time jobs, more extracurriculars, more screen time, and less interest in hanging together. Designate one hour a week to hanging together with a collection of board or card games. And last, but definitely not least, **have a leisurely bath.** No directions required, except: lock the door.

Mama Includes the Kids in Her Fun

Yes, I know you're spending every day with your kids, and you try to spin their educational stuff in a fun way. You have a focus, a goal, an agenda. Why not include the kids when you want to let your hair down too?

> Why not include the kids when you want to let your hair down too?

Occasionally, when you do not need to be alone, or you're trying to incorporate a little self-care because the option of alone time is not available, include the kids. Shift gears.

Spa Day with the kids. Is it just my kids or do everyone's kids make their spas? Cucumber sparkly water, cucumber slices for puffy eyes, warmed bathrobes and towels, foot bowls of Epsom saltwater, facial scrubs, and massages on mattresses pulled to the floor with lotion for backrubs. Hello, inexpensive spa!

Audiobooks. With all those read alouds I read all those years, even I was tired of listening to my own voice. I sampled Audible myself this summer. This was an excellent addition to a summer night spent gazing at the stars through the open screen in our tent, no flashlight required. You can find audiobooks from the library for free or subscribe to Epic as well.

Movie Night. The generations are shifting our kids' viewing practices. My kids are not as interested in movies. (Welcome, YouTube! Sad face emoji.) I love movies, stories, and how stories are told. I love comedy as it helps me see what is true without wallowing in its harshness. I love watching dramatic dips into others' lives so I can glean wisdom without the trial. Once a week I try to convince them with kettle popcorn, tacos and queso, or gummy candies and a scoop of ice cream.

Nature Walks. I know not everyone lives on a homestead twenty minutes outside a cozy mountainside town. Getting outside is easy for me because the chickens need to be released to free-range, the puppy needs attention, and the garden needs weeding. I go out because the downstairs gym with a treadmill and elliptical machine has no appeal for me. I go outside because I feel most alive surrounded by the creation in which we were meant to exist. Do I sound like a proselytizing crunchie girl? Don't sprinkle nutritional yeast on your salad for me but get outside your four walls with your kids.

Play games. Games you like. Don't even get me started on the value of chess; I recognize the benefit to games, but entice me to play chess? No thanks. I'll play Mastermind, Rummy, Rummoli, or Battleship. Playing games together creates memories and tells your kids, you want to have fun together.

Cook together. There is a magical thing that happens a few years after the kids are taught to cook, they become invaluable additions to the household function. They get so talented in the kitchen they can even outcook you (truth: no one does pastry like my daughter). Cooking can be fun as an activity together. Turn on a Spotify playlist, give everyone a special drink, and prepare an enjoyable meal together.

Be intentional about having fun with your kids.

CARING FOR MAMA'S COMMUNITY

We're different and yet, we need each other. We weren't built to live as hermits.

Mama's Community

When we're doing something atypical like homeschooling, we're eager to find that tribe, share the load, and have someone to share the experience. We want to be part of a group that feels like we're doing life similarly and that we have resources available when challenges arise.

Homogeneous communities don't exist. That community of homeschoolers that thinks like you, parents like you, homeschools like you, and values what you value? They don't exist in great number. That we would independently homeschool our children and step out of mainstream screams we don't care if we are just like everyone else.

Organizations have challenges agreeing on the same vision. Countries have difficulties deciding on their financial and political focus. Homogeneity doesn't exist in boardrooms, community planning committees, political parties, or anywhere else, despite the desire for that perfect connection.

Even in churches, homogeneity doesn't exist. Members don't understand God the same way. It's challenging enough to get members to agree on pew colour, let alone agree on a statement of faith.

And in the most significant unified relationship, marriage, homogeneity still doesn't exist. Spouses don't think identically. Sometimes we have different political views, diverse worldviews, and different opinions on which brand of peanut butter should be purchased (PS

Adam's is the right answer).

We're different and yet, we need each other. We weren't built to live as hermits. In a world where self-sufficiency and individuality are prized and encouraged, we still can't function alone.

For years, I had a fascination with self-sufficiency. I thought I'd want to live off-grid, no electricity, eat my own vegetables and fruits, milk my own goats, process my own chickens, grow my own grain, and live in a tiny house with my four children. I made a detailed plan.

My husband reminded me we would have three teenage girls in that tiny house. And that he couldn't be more than fifteen minutes from town as an anesthesia doctor. We settled for 500 square feet per child twenty minutes out of town, with electricity, our septic field, and water well. Now that I tend sixteen chickens, oversee an 800 square foot garden, start my own seedlings in January, can pickles, jams and sauces, freeze fruits and veggies, bake bread, forage in season, share a cow, and know how to build a fire from hand-chopped firewood, I have

> Homogeneity doesn't exist…despite the desire for that perfect connection.

learned that self-sufficiency is an incredibly effort-filled goal. Self-sufficiency *begone!*

Community enables me...

➤ To share a tenth of a cow, so I enjoy its milk but don't have to milk Clara twice daily.

➤ To enjoy Wi-Fi and electricity.

➤ To fix the washing machine when it breaks down.

➤ To help remove a tree that fell on the electric shed.

➤ To clear snow from our private road.

➤ To still eat kale and blueberries and peaches when my garden and orchard haven't produced well.

➤ To have neighbours who'll look out for my roaming Great Pyrenes puppy when she gets off her lead.

Community helps us to parent. Sometimes we don't know what to do. We've got an issue with our child that we haven't dealt with before. There weren't family rules enacted for this issue because it never dawned on us that our child would challenge them. This is parenting. We decide how we'll engage the challenge. Now's the time we need community. We need a variety of people to voice their thoughts, to give us perspective, and to provide us with ideas we hadn't considered.

We're busy with our own family, and there is barely enough time to bring the meat out of the freezer for dinner, pick up our daughter from ballet on time, and keep the radar on that toddler. Community can help.

Share driving. When the kids initially saw where we would build our home, their reaction was: "Why out here?" I determined they would leave one day soon, but I would not. We have accommodated for the out of town experience by driving. A lot. Driving to town more than once a day, transporting kids to dance and theatre and choirs and soccer and curling, and you fill in the blank. Take turns sharing the driving with another family if you can.

Have fun with other families. Learn about other people's values and perspectives by intentionally mixing with people you think might not think like you. You can do this by sharing in local homeschool groups. For example, use Facebook threads to invite other families to a planned field trip. A great way to meet new people.

Develop community mentors. Know your children's mentors. My kids had a run of years learning violin under the influence of a renowned concertmaster. When the last child wanted to hang up her violin bow, I was tempted to offer adoption papers to the teacher. "Please convince her the violin will make her life complete." He had a positive influence on the kids that I didn't want to relinquish. He was orderly, expectant of their regular practicing, warm and encouraging, yet still no-nonsense. He was part of our consistent weekly routine for years. We occasionally cross paths, but he is no longer a weekly staple. I am thankful for his presence and his impact.

> ...but if you present your authentic self, you'll build community.

Create homeschool family connections. Whatever the activity you prefer, just throw out an on-line invitation, and interested people will come. Homeschool not-back-to-school picnics, Christmas tea, and cookie exchanges or summer year-end parties are all great reasons to connect. Homeschool park days and homeschool theatre projects have been part of our regular routine over the years.

Recognize the community right in front of you. Whom do you see all the time? Researchers say you're most likely to build community around the people you see the most regularly. This might mean the FedEx guy, the mailperson, the grocery clerk, the piano teacher, the farm supply guy, or the choir director. These people may not be the ones you instinctively think of as friends, but if you present your authentic self, you'll build community.

Create homeschool support nights. Invite homeschool mamas for coffee, or a potluck mom's brunch or wine 'n cheese night, or to meet a community homeschool support person. You might discover a playmate for your child, or a true friend you connect with.

Search for mentor-like employers. Many homeschooled families enable their kids to find jobs in the early years. We have a lot more time on our hands, and we tend toward industry and entrepreneurialism. These employers are incredible mentors that offer a fresh perspective on the world.

Swap kids. Sometimes sending the kids to a friend is a great way to share community. Then a week later, bring their kids to your place. A couple of friends my son regularly connects with share some of his interests: chess and Lego. They bring all sorts of other benefits to my son's world: a passion for a new reading genre, skills in carpentry (one summer, they spent time building a wooden raft for the river), and discussions on all sorts of topics as they are well-read, intelligent boys. (PS You may need to add noise-reducing headphones to your budget, but it'll be worth it!)

Sharing a crisis. When you have to head to Emerg with a child, when you head to a counseling appointment on your own, when you take an aging parent to a doctor appointment, or when you deal with other life moments that happen unexpectedly, you will have a built-in community that can help you in a pinch.

Homeschool family community can be built with whomever you choose to surround yourself.

"I've learned that people will forget
what you said,
people will forget what you did,
but people will never forget how you
made them feel."
Maya Angelou

Mama's Partner

What is the unique characteristic of a homeschool marriage? Mama focuses on the children, a delight for the kids, but perhaps in doing so creates a more significant challenge for the marriage. The emotional energy and time expended on those

> Mama focuses on the children...but perhaps in doing so creates a more significant challenge for the marriage.

children can take away emotional energy and effort from her partner. We need to set times aside for just us and our partner, even in the thick of this busy, crazy, mostly happy homeschool life.

Don't forget fun with each other. Most families have children who will leave one day. They venture into the world and try new things, like new jobs, new schools, and then they develop their own social networks and families.

When our kids are younger, we sometimes get bogged down with their constant care needs. It feels like yesterday that our beautiful first baby was colicky, not sleeping through the night till she was ten months old, and even then, she demanded to be held all the time. Then she was three, walking to the cashier with money in hand, expecting the cashier to give her a cookie in exchange. She was annoyed when the cashier said she was cute. Then it felt like the next day, but she was nearly eighteen, and I was watching her walk through the airport security so she could backpack Mexico for five months. Yesterday, she and her dad boarded a plane to fly across the country, where she'll start her freshman year in social sciences. They do indeed grow up.

> You and your partner are the engines that move your family train, so the engine must be fueled.

When they do grow up, their dad and I will sit together in a tranquil, possibly tidy room, not teach fractions, not drive to soccer practice, not, hopefully, still manage kids' squabbles. We will have built a lifetime of stories together. Will we know how to spend the next twenty to forty years?

Create alone-time rituals. Whether you watch our favourite tv shows, hike, enjoy an after-dinner drink, play Scrabble, or read a book together — no matter what you do, practice doing something together, learn to enjoy each other's' interest, so you won't be strangers or lack common interests once the kids are gone.

Maintain date nights. It might not come as a

surprise that the homeschool lifestyle doesn't boast increased date time. Hanging with the kiddos 24/7ish makes date night a challenge.

You're busy during the day. Your sleep is interrupted. Teenagers get chatty late at night, middlers still wake from bad dreams, and littles, well, there's no predictability with the littles. Extracurricular activities roam the weekly schedule when a family has teenagers. You're in the busiest period of your family history.

You and your partner are the engines that move your family train, so the engine must be fueled. The "little engine that could" CAN'T when it doesn't have a date night.

A date night at home? It's simpler and cheaper, sometimes. If I can get the kids to make steak in the kitchen while we linger over a glass of wine (an excellent reason to teach cooking), then dance to our favourite Spotify playlist, I am content. Maybe you'll hear, "Mom, she's being mean," or when you enter the kitchen, you find an unusual number of dishes. The special memories created between you will be worth the effort.

Splurge on a special night once a month. Dinner at a fine dining restaurant, or even a fast food restaurant, a movie, a theatre or symphony presentation, a hike or cross-country ski along the canal, a walk in the neighbourhood? I would never suggest shopping with my special someone (that would be self-torture), but I've heard of couples wandering through Costco and even dining at sampling stations. At home, ask him to bring you a coffee and make breakfast together.

Trade kids. When the kids were younger, I traded kids with friends for an afternoon. Instead of crossing things off the to-do list, schedule an afternoon with the hubby, then close the curtains and light the candles.

Enlist family support. If you have parents in your area, or siblings without families of their own, ask them if they can look after the kids for a few hours or even a weekend. The time you have separate from your children will enable your connection in a way you may not expect.

Take a weekend without guilt.

Plan a weekend getaway. I recently overheard a homeschool mama ask jokingly (maybe?) if her eleven-year-old was mature enough to look after his three siblings...for the weekend. Might be a bit young, no matter how independent, but I understand her eagerness.

I loved my fortieth birthday when my husband surprised me with a visit from my brother, who lived a few hour's flight away. My husband whisked me to a Michael Bublé concert in San Francisco and my brother looked after the kids for the weekend. These dates are rare occurrences for us, but remarkable memories.

If you get a weekend or week away, take a weekend without guilt. The terms of your homeschool mama agreement are rarely random acts of adult fun. The nurturing you provide your kids can be interrupted, and they will still grow up to be connected to you even if you're not present 24/7.

We get away to really see each other, to clarify, again, what we want in life, in our work aspirations, in our family, and in our relationships.

Ask Dad for homeschool help. Increasingly over our homeschool years, my husband has involved himself in our homeschool days in ways he hadn't early on. Conversations at the table are qualitatively different as we stop to discuss and explain things the kids don't understand. We recognize our responsibility to teach them what we know. His knowledge of politics, government, and economics have been staple discussions with the kids.

Certain kids are more likely to wait till dad comes home to review new math concepts. He shares his love of history, economics, and government with them. He is the go-to financial guy in our home: he likes to learn about stocks, bonds, market shares, bitcoin, and gold prices. He has a unique knowledge of Broadway theatre and 1980s country tunes.

Expect your partner to be interested in their children's education and encourage sharing their interests with their kiddos. Dads always get involved if you homeschool long enough. Just give 'em time.

If your partner is not accustomed to participating at all, let's chat. Maybe your partner arrives home, collapses in front of the tv with a beer, and waits for your call for supper. Then he sits with fork and knife with bated breath until you enter from stage left (the messy kitchen) and provide him his favourite roast and Yorkshire pudding, with chocolate souffle for dessert. Then, while you clean up, you settle the noisy children with their game of pick-up sticks and chutes and ladders while he slinks to his den with a cigar, glass of bourbon, and The New Yorker magazine where he dozes. During his nap, you do the bedtime read-aloud and help the kids recite their prayers, kiss them goodnight and turn out their lights. Then you tidy yourself so you can slide into his den, sit on your partner's lap, and rouse him from his sleep. If this resonates with you, here's your action plan:

➢ Expect him to participate. Homeschooling is a dual-parent thing (if you have the dual-parent thing going on). Your partner is part of the homeschool life with you.

➢ Let him know you need help. He's got his stuff going on and he might think you're killing this homeschool thing or think you don't want him to interfere. Ask him and be specific in your asking.

➢ Ask for specific help. I know, I want my husband to read my mind after twenty years of marriage too. The cult myth isn't a myth: they don't read minds.

➢ Don't watch how he helps. Don't tell him not to throw the baby in the air and play sing-songy games, or stop playing wrestling games with the kiddos, or criticize him for making packaged noodles for dinner, again. If you want him to help, let him help in his way.

➢ When he helps, do some self-care. Don't let yourself walk towards another chore. The laundry will wait. The dishes will wait. Walk yourself to the bathtub with a glass of bubbly and a book, or a café with a friend, or walk outside by yourself.

Whatever is a half-hour happy moment for you, do that.

➤ Ask again. Your partner won't remember what worked for you that one time. He won't likely build that into his routine. Remember, mind reading isn't a thing.

➤ Spoil him. And of course, make him that roast beef and Yorkshire puddings and tell him to put his feet up with his favourite beer and let him fall asleep to his favourite magazine while you take care of your family by yourself too. He's a homeschool dad with a world outside his family, and he also needs self-care.

Get to know him. I know you KNOW him but get to know him more deeply. Enneagram, Myers-Briggs, or whatever the personality profiling approach will help you to understand him better. Learn to observe him as a separate entity, because he is an independent person outside your family too. This enables you to recognize his strengths, allows you to be objective about his struggles, and helps you gain clarity on the interpersonal

...he might think you're killing this homeschool thing or think you don't want him to interfere.

challenges you may have together.

Decide what goals each of you has for marriage. We human beings want to be affirmed deeply and understood by someone, many someones preferably, but one special someone. If our goal is to be understood by someone, it means we'll have to reciprocate and try to appreciate the other. Easy to write on a page, not so easy to practice every day.

Find a therapist if you don't know how to solve something. Objectivity and perspective are worth their weight in gold, or cash, as it may be.

Remember, your kids are in the front row. Kids get a front-row seat to the circus, I mean, their parent's marriage. Whether you argue in front of the kids or not, your kids are routinely soaked in the tea of their parent's relationship. They recognize when one parent is upset with the other. They recognize when dad is mad at mom. They recognize when mom is unreasonable. Or when both parents are ignoring each other. They see when mom and dad are enjoying a conversation when they're being flirtatious in the kitchen or talking sweetly on the sofa. Kids get the front row seat, good and bad, entertaining or disturbing. Marriage 101: the kids' first training in relationship.

You brought you into the relationship and you will unravel issues staring at you in the mirror. No matter where you're at in marriage, your kids are absorbing, watching, and learning your relational habits, whether they be useful habits, or not-so-useful habits.

Even if our marriages end in divorce, our kids can watch us triumph over hardship, watch us transform unhealthy habits into healthy habits, and watch us heal, learn, grow, and make good stuff out of hard stuff.

Accept your imperfections: own them and do something about them. Be real about your relationship.

"It is a truth universally acknowledged, that a single man in possession of a good fortune, must be in want of a wife." Jane Austen, Pride and Prejudice

Mama's Friends

Is it just me, or when someone asks about the kids' socialization, are you also thinking to yourself, "What about MY socialization?"

We need our own homeschool world and our own homeschool girlfriends. We can find online support easily, but real moms in real time are a powerful presence. Sometimes we need cheerleaders. Someone to tell us if we want to keep homeschooling, we can do it. Sometimes we have an issue with a child we haven't had before. We need a variety of people to voice their opinions so we can gain perspective or give us ideas we hadn't considered. Sometimes we just need to hear that other mamas get exasperated, exhausted, and extended, just like us.

Mamas need mamas. We are independent and capable of homeschooling our children, but we are not lone islands. Nurturing friendships enables connection and satisfies the desire to know and be known. We need to share this journey with others. When we share, we build our community: by being known, understanding others, and enabling meaningful family connections. Maybe we even create mentorships for our children. We can create pseudo-families when we don't have family near us.

> So, put the effort in and you'll quickly discover similarities, because humanity is a common experience.

Accept and build a community where you're at. Once I thought I wanted a community of homeschoolers that thought like me, parented like me, homeschooled like me, and valued stuff I value. No one is the same, but homeschoolers are especially not so as they confidently chose to step out of the mainstream. We all came to homeschool for different reasons, and we maintain homeschooling for various reasons.

Expand your friendships outside the familiar. Be willing to connect with others that might not, at first glance, feel like your tribe. Nurture friendships that are water skiing experiences. If you haven't tried water skiing, imagine this: sitting in a cold lake with your knees bent, trying to balance skis in the swaying waves, holding tightly to the bar attached to the boat, because the boat is about to take you skimming along the waves. The waves are exhilarating. At first glance, this didn't seem like something you'd want to do, so potentially scary. These connections might require effort, but they are also exhilarating.

Some friendships are comfort blankets with similar values and parenting approaches. Some friendships are like traveling to a foreign country with varied perspectives. Instead of paying for plane flights to a foreign land, if we're willing to listen and engage authentically, we can get to know people with all sorts of perspectives (and at just the price of a coffee). Someone who might appear different at first glance might not be so different from us.

Each person that crosses our paths has

something unique to offer. So, put the effort in and you'll quickly discover similarities, because humanity is a common experience. Seven billion people common.

Vulnerability is required to connect. We can't just sit in a crowd and observe and hope others will want to invite us to their home for coffee. When we are vulnerable, when we are real, not trying to be something we're not, we can make those connections.

Know how you relate. Meyer's Briggs thinks I'm an extrovert. Maybe so, but I think barely so. I genuinely enjoy people, listening to their stories, and sharing what we know about life, but I also need restorative quiet, walking my puppy on the canal, sitting with a pen, or quietly reading a book.

Learn how to make friends. I've spent a lifetime moving nineteen times before I was twenty — so I learned most people aren't threatening, and we can connect with anyone if we do this one thing: listen.

Wanna make a fast friend? Listen intently to the person in front of you. Be interested in others' experiences, in how they see their world, or in what they enjoy doing. Every human that crosses our path has something to offer each of us. When a new person is in your presence, take notice, listen, and learn.

Not everyone is my best friend, so I don't necessarily want to share my deepest darkest secrets with them. I could choose to take that risk, though. I can build long, true friendships if I risk being the real me, being vulnerable at times, and consistently spending time with them.

Recognize your idiosyncrasies. I know how to introduce myself unobtrusively in a group, though this is a learned skill for me. From my insecurities, I either didn't speak at all, or I came across too outspoken. Somewhere in my relational learning, I realized everyone is nervous to connect with new people and just being myself was the fastest way of connecting the real me with someone new. Present the fake me and even if they liked me, I wouldn't feel connected to them.

> Present the fake me, and even if they liked me, I wouldn't feel connected to them.

Are homeschool mamas extroverted or introverted? Both, of course. Perhaps because we spend so much time with our children, some of us may not be as extroverted as we once were, or even more introverted than we once were because we are comfortable and content in our own worlds.

Calling all introverts. Even if you're not an extrovert, people need people, so if you're not connected with people you feel supported by, you need to build stronger connections. The one thing I've learned about making friends is that everyone needs friends, extrovert or introvert. Just because we're introverted doesn't mean we can or should do life without others. Make sure you're connected with people that know the true you and are available when you really need them.

I've got a virtual homeschool friend who has spoken more into my life than any other. She's parented five. They're all grown up now. She's been through years and years of curriculum planning, and even unschooling, learning to do homeschool right and letting go of the notion that you can "do it right." She's told me to relax. She's told me to pay a little more attention. She's the coach from the sidelines, repeating her mantra, "Live graciously, love honestly, write bravely."

Direct from her book, *A Gracious Space,* I share (with permission) Julie Bogart's words with you:

> Don't overthink. Do you want to do a good job of parenting?

Think less about how to shape your kids into world-changers and more about how to bring a wide world to your family to reshape them.

Think less about turning your kids into responsible mini-adults and more about how to ensure they have a childhood.

Think more about how much energy children invest in what they love and less about what they fail to do.

Think more about each child's natural aptitudes and less about each child's deficiencies.

Think less about the future and more about today -- this moment.

Think less about expert advice and more about your hunches.

Think more about your children than the Famous People who write about them.

Think less about disciplinary tactics and more about live and let live.

Think less of yourself (your power to impact who your children become) and more about the innate ability of genetics, culture, language, and nationality.

Allow yourself to be in awe; disallow anxiety. Think more about what you can control (your own character and maturity) and less about what you can't (your children's character and maturity).

Think more of your child's responsibility to grow up to be who he or she is, and less of your ability to make some imagined outcome happen.

Think only of your responsibility to provide possibilities and opportunities, and less of your obligation to guarantee outcomes (to anyone: the government, your spouse, your extended family, yourself).

Let yourself off the hook--you are limited. Celebrate your limits. Let your kids off the hook -- they are limited. Enjoy their limits.

Think about all the signs of maturity, character, intelligence, and heart you do see. Think less about the recklessness, slipshod work ethic, bickering, and lack of academic progress that reminds you they are still minors.

Think more of yourself than you usually

do. You are enough, you have the right kids, you know what it means to love and educate them. You do it every day.

Think less of the revered friends and experts. They are not you. They do what they do. They don't have your kids. They can't parent for you. They shouldn't live in your head.

Think more about developing thinkers (people who engage ideas) and less about getting your kids through an education (people who pass classes).

Think more of home education when you are at home, defending it to yourself, and protect it less to other people.

You do know what you're doing. The tweaks and changes you make are validations of your vision, not invalidations of past choices. You are growing alongside your children, becoming an educator as you go.

Think more of your journey as a homeschooler, and less about what your kids are learning.

If you value your growth, you'll learn to appreciate your kids' growth.

If you love what you are learning about education and learning, your kids will find some version of that lifestyle for themselves. It's contagious.

If you are undistracted by the flaws in your system, personality, finances, and home life and think more about how to become intimate with a subject area that fascinates you, your entire life (including homeschool and children) will flourish.

Don't overthink this one. Stay the course, learn, grow, share, trust.

You are less important in the whole scheme of things than you realize, and you are far more valuable in the moment-to-moment day by day than you appreciate.

Both are true. **Don't overthink it.**

Who wouldn't want a homeschool girlfriend to speak those things into your life?

I've learned so much from you, Julie. Someday, I hope to meet you. The tea kettle is always ready!

Mama's Kids

Spend intentional time with the kids. Say what? Schedule time with my kids? I'm a homeschooling mama. I'm with my kids 24-7 unless they're at dance, curling, choir, playdates, youth group, gymnastics, or their Grandma's house. Why are we talking about spending more time with our kids?

We might have an organized homeschool routine, but that doesn't mean we're available to look our child in the eye and listen to him share the details of his Minecraft building or watch her forty-five-minute Barbie wedding ceremony.

They might have access to our homeschool mama faces, but they don't necessarily have our heartfelt mama's attention. Nor can mamas always provide that attention. Our kids need these gold star, connecting moments. We need them too. It's one of

> Teenagers seem to be notoriously available right before their bedtime.

the reasons we're doing what we're doing, so we need to find ways to make sure we include fun with our children. We need fun with each of our children.

How to make intentional time? Depending on

how many kids you have, you could schedule one-on-one time with a child once a week. Or fifteen minutes once a day with each child. Or once a day, half an hour before bed. Whatever way you do it, make sure it doesn't feel like another thing on your to-do list. And do it with regularity. Do that activity with just one child. Be eye contact connectable.

What to talk about. Learn to lead in conversations without appearing to lead into conversations. Ask about their interests. Ask them to show you their creative art, favourite Barbie, Lego creations, or room décor. These are moments you don't want to miss. (You likely had a family for these moments.) You will hear more about your kids' interests at this moment than at any time you're buying groceries, doing a spelling lesson, or checking their math.

Bring the kids into your world. Early in my gardening years, I brought my kids into the garden, to till, to weed, to seed, and to harvest. Enough years went by, and they understood that dropping seeds, pulling carrots, snipping beans, and twisting zucchini were chores, not fun. I could no longer entice them. I relish moments when we're standing in the garden, even if just to chat with them.

Teenagers seem to be notoriously available

right before their bedtime. These discussions can often be inconvenient timing as we are just winding down, since teenagers can be clamshells in spilling their real thoughts and feelings, or sometimes no words at all. These truth serum midnight hours are so useful to maintain connection.

Back to the fun. Search for activities you like to do with each child. You don't have to learn the art of chess even if your son loves it. You could play your favourite childhood game with them or go for a bike ride in the evening. You could throw a blanket in the backyard and stargaze in August to watch the Perseids. You could take them for coffee, then walk through an art gallery. You could play in a trampoline gym together.

Listen to their hearts and **build your memories** while you have the chance to make them.

"Life is not measured by the number of breaths you take,
but by the moments that take your breath away."
Maya Angelou

THE CARE AND KEEPING OF THE HOMESCHOOL HOME

Household organization and mental organization enables more purposeful living.

Organization Breeds Freedom
I'd like to be your Marie Kondo for homeschool, if you'll let me. As I've informally polled moms about their goal in home organization,

I've learned that not every mom wants to learn to cook, clean and housekeep like their 1950s foremothers. I understand. We don't have to decorate the home, we don't have to make homemade meals, we don't have to do anything we don't want to. (Except if we can't afford a housekeeper, a cook, and a nanny: probably not many of us.)

If you are rolling your eyes at a section about organization breeding freedom, then just flip past this section. However, in those informal polls, I've learned that most homeschool moms are eager to get their world organized.

Organization sounds like a make-work project. A lot of work, in the beginning, but household organization and mental organization enables more purposeful living. Way leads onto way.

Organization requires consistent effort. If you put organization into almost everything you do, with regular practice, you find mental freedom, purpose, and more time.

What is essential in your days? Is it important for you to schedule a full day of studies? Is it important that you have a tidy home at all times? Is it important for you to visit the dentist once or twice a year? Is it important for you to preplan doctor checkups or book appointments in advance? Are you going to include a date night once a decade, or is it on the calendar regularly?

Fast track your organization by time auditing everything you do. The simplest way to organize your days is to write down everything you want to accomplish in your day. Guesstimate how much time each activity requires and write them into your daytimer in fifteen-minute increments. (Some of these activities will take more than fifteen-minute blocks, so add extra time.)

Analyze your time audit. When you've scheduled everything that you want to include in your day, from self-care to laundry to math games to dinner prep to driving to soccer practice, pay attention to the *actual time* each of those activities take. Check the clock. Scheduling every activity will make your schedule realistic and achievable. When you build in enough shoulder time (or breathing

> If you put organization into everything you do, with regular practice, you find mental freedom, purpose, and more time.

space) around each of those activities, you won't feel stressed, and you won't push the kids out the door. (And if you're like me, you'll realize you've planned too much. So delete, delete, delete.)

Kondofy your household organization:

➢ **Create a predictable housecleaning routine.** If you've got a predictable cleaning routine, you don't have to be overwhelmed by disorganization. You associate certain days with specific activities. Saturday morning is household cleaning. Friday afternoon is laundry day. Every activity that's important to you needs to be slotted into a consistent routine. (I'll add here, you won't do everything like clockwork, so expect life to get in the way. But when you implement routine, you'll get that list done most of the time.)

➢ **Create a predictable homeschool routine.** If you know each morning before studies, you'll have circle time (also called a family meeting when you have teenagers), you can be flexible about the content. The kids will know circle time starts at 8:30, so you won't have to corral them for a discussion before the day. (Well, eventually, when you've done this 4932 days).

➢ **Keep a household chore list.** Expect everyone to pitch in. Lower your cleanliness expectations when a child is learning a new task (keep in mind, someone will always be learning a new task if you have more than one kiddo). And if you can, lower your cleanliness standards; if you can't, plan reasonably.

➢ **Schedule the household chores.** I don't enjoy Friday afternoons because I know after a solid study week, I will do laundry. I do love knowing my bedroom sheets are warm and clean for the weekend, however. (FYI it took me almost two decades to wash my sheets every week, so if you think that's incomprehensible, then don't do it!) The key to clean sheets is to put this task on my schedule.

➢ **Keep a running grocery list.** You'll always be running out of something. Plan a specific day of the week, or day of the month, to head to the grocery store. Don't be rigid in your menu plans but anticipate you are indeed going to have another meal today, so plan for routine grocery shopping. (Consult my menu planning section for more detail.)

➢ **Preplan menus and maintain meal and snack routines.** Meals don't have to be fancy. Keep the menu simple, but balanced. Repeat seven meals until you're tired of them. Then you'll always have easy food prep at the top of your mind.

My issue with minimalism: quite simply, *you need stuff.* Even if you decide to put everything meaningful into one backpack and travel the world, you still need stuff. (Maybe very little stuff, but you need an extra pair of underwear and a toothbrush for sure.) Maybe your long-term goal is to travel the world with a backpack. Until then, you probably need a few kitchen things, a couple sets of sheets and a table and chairs, a mattress, oh, and cutlery. There's nothing wrong with stuff that has a purpose. You need stuff to do your purpose. I think this is the reason people want to get rid of stuff: they haven't determined their purpose. When we become clear on our purpose, we'll become clear on what we need to own for that purpose.

Tips for your homeschool organization:

➤ **Use a calendar.** Use a monthly calendar just for homeschool academics and another just for household appointments.

➤ **Build a daily practice of consulting that calendar** (no use having a calendar if you're not using it). If you check the calendar for five minutes before you start your day, right after lunch, or maybe after all the studies are complete, you'll maintain organization.

➤ **Once a week, set aside a time to plan.** Determine what you want to do for the week, your menu plan, your grocery list, your kids' study activities, your extracurriculars, your social visits, your self-care. Jot it all down. (There will come a time that your planning won't have to be written. The kids will have the routine written into their subconscious, and so will you.)

➤ **Record the kids' completed study activities as they do them.** Write those activities as you do them, not as you plan to do them for these reasons: First, you'll remember you did them more easily and second, you'll gain a keener sense of how learning opportunity translates into an actual education. Win-win.

➤ **Colour code your children's academic calendars.** Use a blue pen for language arts, orange for history, green for science, purple for foreign languages, red for math, and individual colours for each of your kids' extracurricular activities.

➤ **Maintain a calendar just for teenagers.** Sorry toddler moms, your life gets busier when you have teenagers (a different kind of busy). When kids grow up, their lives get complicated and hectic. If you can find a magnetic fridge calendar with erasable markers, have the kids write their activities in a colour code each Sunday evening. This will keep you from wondering where you're supposed to be driving or where you're supposed to be picking up the kids.

➤ **Practice flexibility but maintain routine.** If you have preplanned what books or subject areas you want to study, you don't have to prepare extra effort the night before your studies. You know what books you'll be reading and what topics you will focus on. You can create a loose schedule that suggests specific topics on certain days or plan for an hour each day for history or science. Hold the routine loosely, so if it breaks (*when* it breaks), your expectations aren't dashed.

➤ **Organization doesn't mean lesson plans for forty weeks.** Sure, do lesson plans if that's your thing. Don't worry about spelling practice for the word "burnout" now though, because you're going to learn it soon enough. Alternatively, learn what elements of language arts can be useful for your child's communication skills as adults. Follow a math curriculum for one child, and you'll learn what elements of mathematics they need. Pursue your kids' interests and passions in anything history or science and write them down. Come up with related topics you can explore throughout the year and pursue them as your interest flows. Practice going with the flow of your plans, and you will be much happier.

➢ **Keep a portfolio.** At the end of the year, write a portfolio for each of your kids. Yes, this is a lot of work. However, you will be amazed at how much they have accomplished and how much they have been exposed to, and you will be in awe of their fantastic education. This will inform you about their learning, interests and aptitudes. It will equip you with perspective and freedom on what an education is anyway.

➢ **Cluster errands and extracurriculars.** If you're going out anyway, and the kids are at an activity, this is your time to book appointments. Then you can get all your stuff done.

Expect your organizational strategies to change from year to year. Each year you learn more about your kids and how they learn. You may have learned you don't want to start studies until you've had quiet time in the morning. You may have learned how long it takes you to do history with the kids. You've learned whether you or your child even want to do history. Over the last year, you might have had an illness, you might have had to look after a parent, you have struggled with your partner, or you may have learned you have a special needs child — so many reasons to throw a wrench into your well-intended plans. All these scenarios have informed you about your family. Adjust your organizational strategy as needed.

Once a year, take stock. What do you want to include in your life? Focus on those activities. You will focus your efforts, your energy and your time toward the things you want to be doing, only if you know what you want to be doing. (See the Taking Stock section for detailed questions to organize your life once a year.)

Menu Plan & Tips

I began menu planning when I was a little girl. I kid you not. I thought hamburgers would be a weekly necessity for my someday family, so I created an alphabetic list of hamburgers. A for apple burgers, B for breakfast burgers, C for carrot burgers. Yikes. Good thing I didn't use that one.

Meal planning sounds like a smart idea if you weren't already homeschooling all day, or didn't have a slew of little kids, or didn't have a lot of extracurriculars. I know menu planning is a lot of effort, but it is worth the effort.

Plan and you are more likely to make healthier choices, you'll always have ingredients on hand, and you'll spend less. When my eldest daughter left home for the first time, she expressly thanked me for having a stocked pantry. Jaw drop.

Meal planning requires effort in the beginning. I think the process of cooking is enjoyable when kids want to eat what you're making. Practice with the same recipes until you have them locked in your brain, no longer cooking from recipes, and then move on to something new. Do this often enough and you can stare at a piece of frozen fish and know you can make fish tacos, baked fish with rice — or move onto something the kids want to eat, because fish isn't on that list.

There have been times I forgot to pull something from the freezer in the morning, then realized I would be in town over dinnertime. There have been times I couldn't prep a meal before I left the house for afternoon extracurriculars and had to pick up something.

There have been times I realized I had lots of leftovers and didn't need to make another meal. Often enough, I've ignored my original dinner plan altogether and instead said, "What can we eat from the fridge?"

Shopping is simpler when a menu plan is prepped in advance. Prep meals ready for a week. I'm not going to suggest you prepare enough food for a month over a weekend. I don't love cooking that much (but if you do, carpe cook-em!) If you do weekly menu planning, you don't have to panic an hour before a meal; you don't have to microwave frozen hamburger in hopes you don't partially cook it and still have raw meat. You don't have to run a steady stream of warm water over a frozen package that will be ready tomorrow.

Keep a consistent weekly plan. One day a week, consistently make chicken, fish, eggs, beans, beef, or pork. This means you have two days a week for leftovers, and everyone knows there are leftovers in the fridge. So why waste the money? My weekly plan looks like this: Monday Fish night. Tuesday Chicken night. Wednesday Vegetarian night. Thursday Random night. Friday Fun food. Saturday Leftovers night. Sunday Fancy Feast.

Keep it simple. You might be overspending if

you're buying that jar of roasted red peppers. These items might be delicious, but five extra dollars in the grocery budget in a week seems like a hit if you're using that ingredient every few months, and the kids don't like it anyway.

Don't intricately menu plan. **Buy accompanying veggies based on season for both nutrition and lower cost. Use the veggies you have; asparagus doesn't have to pair with smoked salmon** *(because you know, smoked salmon is a typical homeschool meal)*. If I have five different meals planned, I don't have to coordinate my vegetables like a restaurant. Buy veggies on sale, then add whatever is found in the fridge.

Always have go-to vegetables the kids will eat. You know, carrots and celery, or whatever they like.

Don't **make breakfast.** Provide what your kids need. When they can, teach them to make hot cereal, so when it's the day before grocery day, and there's no bread, cold cereal, or yoghurt in the pantry, they know how to prep oatmeal.

Make a morning kitchen routine: pull frozen meat from the freezer when you're making morning coffee (a tip from someone who doesn't own a microwave). Alternatively, throw something into a crockpot or Instapot while you're making coffee.

Occasionally critique your meals for nutrition. Left to my own appetite, I would eat Miss Vickie's every night. Umm, I know better, but my appetite does not. Yet though I know better, it's still too easy to grab that bag in that aisle. I've had many dietary tweaking moments over the years.

> Left to my own appetite, I would eat Miss Vickie's [potato chips] every night.

I know I should be eating coldwater fish twice a week, and you'd think I would do that being as close to the coast as we are, but I don't have eager fish eaters, so I don't. Once a week, we eat fish. (Twice a week if I've forgotten to pull out meat from the freezer, because frozen fish cooks quickly). A regular dietary self-assessment seems appropriate as we're teaching our kids to eat. We're also fueling our mama brains to engage our homeschool worlds with as much energy as we can muster.

Include eggs, beans, and/or lentils once a week. Lighten up the pocketbook and the digestive system by including beans, lentils, and eggs. I prefer curried lentils and rice for lunch with summer-made chutneys. Beans and lentils are inexpensive, easy to prep, and if you prepare plenty on Monday, that meal will last for a few days.

Make food prep a fun family tradition. Make pizza on Friday nights, pour the kids a glass of sparkling beverage, and you a glass of wine. Pretend you're in Tuscany, while you cook with Giada.

Leftovers are delightful. Assign one evening for leftovers. This will be your saving grace on those frenetic days. Or break from routine on the weekend: to not cook once a week, bravo! (And fewer dishes to wash.) Save leftovers all week, freeze them, and pull them out for one big Saturday evening buffet.

Enjoy Sunday night leisure. Make breakfast for supper. I'm not eager for pancakes myself, but my kids sure are. Or make Sunday a fancy meal, crepes with fruit filling, or a roast beef, mashed potatoes, Yorkshire pudding, and a fruit pie for dessert.

Too much organization can make a mama crazy. Strictly adhering to regimens is not a useful strategy for happy family making. Just as having a flexible educational plan is helpful, mama has got to determine a flexible meal plan too.

➤ Assume you're going to individualize your menu plan for your family.

➤ Assume you are not locked into a meal plan for the next eighteen years.

➤ Assume you're going to buy dinner out unexpectedly.

➤ Assume you're going to have more leftovers than you thought.

➤ Assume you will get invited over for dinner occasionally — or have guests unexpectedly.

Grocery Store Tips

➤ **Go by yourself if you can.** Though grocery shopping isn't an ideal quiet time, it's still separate time from the family. Do not use this time as your fun time (we all know it isn't). But grocery shop alone for maximum enjoyment.

➤ **Teach the kids to shop.** When they must come with you, give them an item or two to fetch, learn about cost comparison, or make a game about guessing prices. Try a treasure hunt for the younger kids.

➢ Meat is likely the most expensive part of your grocery budget. **Include lentils, beans, eggs, and even tofu.** Assume that twice a week, you're not eating meat (unless you're already a vegetarian, then ignore what I just said.)

➢ **Buy on sale.** Stock the pantry with things you regularly use. Chia seeds and pine nuts don't need to be on hand in my home. Pasta, rice, and potatoes do. Buy fish or meat on sale and stick it in the freezer. If you're routinely eating similar foods, you know you're going to eat them again, so plan for that.

➢ **Buy in season.** Seasonal fruit and veggies are less expensive. Don't get fussy about having Brussel sprouts paired with roast beef or green beans with salmon. Use vegetables you have on hand. Keep a bag of precut carrots or snap peas for alternative kid veggies when you're serving the adults rapini.

➢ **Start a small garden.** For a package of $3 seeds, you can eat salad for a summer.

Gardening can significantly reduce your grocery budget.

➢ **Think partitioned plate.** Half veggie, quarter meat, and quarter carbs. Simple.

➢ **Buy expensive ingredients sparingly.** Prepared foods and specialty ingredients like cans of roasted red peppers or European cheeses are more expensive. Organic oranges and produce with thick skins are expensive organic purchases since they naturally repel chemicals.

➢ **Use the same grocery store.** Your mind knows where to find maple syrup in the primary grocery store you use. Go to another store, and they've tucked it somewhere random. Every time you walk past the peanut butter section that will be your reminder to consistently grab it if you run out.

Cooking Tips

Not everyone who homeschools is also Suzy Homemaker. However, I'll introduce you to her: she's me. I'm not the 1950s housewife. I wear yoga pants and my hair doesn't get washed for days. No heels here. I'm not waiting hand and foot on my husband when he arrives home.

There's no smoking jacket and a glass of bourbon (actually, he likes bourbon). And there's no pot roast every night. (I do that on Sunday, ha). Cooking is a developed skill. If you're a skilled chef, your family is blessed. If you can stare at any piece of meat or hold any can in your pantry and know how to make a meal with it, then you have arrived.

Do you want a few cooking tips to make your homeschool world smoother?

➢ **Learn to cook.** But if you don't know how to cook, do you want to learn? The more you learn to cook many things, the easier that aspect will be. There are millions of cookbooks and YouTube cooking channels. Maybe this could be part of your learning plan? Add a glass of vino, turn on a YouTube cooking show, and make learning to cook an entertaining weekly event for you.

➢ **Cook more than you need.** If you're cooking from scratch, make more than one meal. Freeze the rest. Label what you put in the freezer, so you don't have random surprises like chicken broth for lunch, instead of the butternut squash soup you thought you were defrosting.

You'll thank yourself for your extra effort later.

➢ **Teach the kids to cook.** There is no greater freedom than not to have to cook all the time. Let the kids feed you. Let them try cooking when they're younger, when they think cooking is the best thing ever. If they can safely hold a knife, let them learn knife skills. If they can help measure, they can measure. If they're old enough to watch over a burner, they are old enough to cook. If you know they're not ready, then wait. When the kids begin to cook, walk away from the kitchen. Yup, I'm serious (said a mom that likes to direct everything). "Your way" probably is better, but natural learning is the most quickly absorbed learning. When they put too much baking soda in their cupcakes, they will likely never do it again. When they start getting good at food preparation, tell them you'll clean up if they make dinner. Win-win. Teaching kids to cook means you won't have to cook every night for the rest of your parenting days.

➢ **Recreate leftovers.** Leftovers are a mama's best friend. Learn how to turn a basic beef roast into fajitas. Learn how to turn baked salmon to salmon cakes.

Learn how to transform chicken thighs into chicken pot pie. Learn how to slice pork chops into stir-fries. Learn to recreate.

➢ **Purchase plastic food containers.** If you're driving your kids to extracurriculars, designate specific coloured containers for each person and make weekly takeaway meals. You'll spend less and you'll eat better. Choose foods that the kids want to eat. Possible homemade takeaway options: chicken Caesar wraps, pizza (of course), veggie burgers, pasta, and quesadillas. Anything that's not too challenging to eat in a car outside Walmart or on a park bench.

➢ **Cook flexibly.** We are taught in Home economics class that Caesar salad complements lasagna, that biscuits and gravy are best with grits, and that roast chicken and tiny roasted potatoes pairs well with sauvignon blanc. But am I the only homeschool mom that has other stuff to do than just cook a meal, again? Just feed the kids. Prep a veggie offering to fill half a plate, prep a quarter plate filled with carbs and include a quarter plate of protein. Tada. 1-2-3- magic. Be flexible.

> ➤ **Takeaway Tips.** For years after we had moved to a new town, we drove a half-hour to our extracurriculars. I was unaccustomed to this routine, so we ate out four times a week. Eating out regularly eats up monthly grocery budgets fast.

House Cleaning

I'll tell you a secret my children don't know: the moment my youngest leaves home, I'm hiring a housekeeper. I'm not wasting my time washing floors or vacuuming sofa cushions anymore. I will have completed twenty-six years of household management, so onward and upward. In the meantime, I'm teaching my kids to houseclean.

My mom didn't let my fiancé and I sit in the living room because the carpet had just been vacuumed. And raked. Yes, I said raked. And every bathtub or sink in my childhood home had to be dried out after use. None of these practices I maintain in my home, but I've been trained by the best.

Still, I am one of those homeschool moms capable of keeping a relatively clean and tidy home during the homeschool year. I won't try to convert you if you're not. I tend to think people aren't convertible unless they want to be, so you decide.

Are you a Marie Kondo housecleaner? I won't hold things in my hands and thank them for their efforts, but I do regularly rid myself of my belongings. When you get rid of stuff you don't want or need, you feel lighter. When you know where everything is, you waste less time. Make sure everything you own has a purpose and a goal. That purpose and goal might be to remember your Grandma, since her stash of letters to her new husband is a sweet memory; that is a good enough reason to keep those letters if they are

> This reminds me I should probably go downstairs to unclutter the storage room.

valuable to you. Just be intentional what you keep and why you keep it. PS This reminds me I should probably go downstairs to unclutter the storage room.

When you keep things tidy, your mind feels tidier. Declutter your world, and you declutter your mind. *Cleaning is simply preparing your stuff for another use at another time.* All your things have a purpose. Everything you clean or tidy is a way to prepare it for bringing joy, memories, and use to your family. Remember this so cleaning won't feel like a waste of time.

If you're new to this homeschool thing, be prepared. Your home will be messier. Expect to find pencils everywhere but in the homeschool zone. Expect to find pencil sharpeners and erasers under sofa cushions. Expect to have a permanent zone in the kitchen for science experiments. Expect dyes, slime, and unknown substances to be found in random containers around the house. Expect to determine a location to pour noxious substances outside your home. Expect eraser shreds on the kitchen table or highlighter and marker messes on that table. Expect walls never to be simultaneously clean again. Expect books to overtake surfaces and floors to look unswept (though they were swept after breakfast). You're living in these four walls all day long so accept they aren't staying clean.

When given an informal poll on how homeschool mamas approach their house cleaning tasks, these moms responded like this:

➢ Fifty-eight said, "We complete basic maintenance daily."

➢ Fifty-five said, "We give kids jobs as needed, but the kids don't have assigned routine chores."

➢ Eleven said, "We clean "fire extinguisher style": quick, someone's coming to visit!"

➢ Nine said, "I cannot have things out of place. I need peace of mind. Call me OCD."

➢ Five said, "I clean once a week. Basics are covered with or without kids' help."

➢ Three said, "We call it an enchanted home, so why tidy and why clean?"

➢ Two said, "If I pull out the vacuum, the kids ask, Who is coming over?"

Establish a daily household routine. A household activity a day keeps the social worker away. Essential daily maintenance will keep the mess from getting too real. Just fifteen minutes before studies begin or fifteen minutes before dinner. If you want to keep on top of things, you need to maintain a routine.

Clean once a week. I clean Friday afternoon or Saturday morning. My teenage girls prefer Friday afternoon so they can sleep in on Saturday morning. Choose a day and be consistent.

Do cleaning together. If they can clean, and household cleaning is important to you, you can all share in that activity. Do you want to counteract the kids' tendency towards entitlement? Housecleaning will help. If your kids are physically incapable of doing a chore, obviously that chore is not for them. If they can do the task, but not perfectly do the task, lower your mama expectations and watch them learn. Assume the child has a six-month practice period to learn the task. Join them in their training, and when they do a good enough job, they can do it on their own.

If you can do it, hire help. If you are at the end of a pregnancy, have a challenging pregnancy, are awake every night with babies or toddlers, have any illness or trauma affecting the family, if you have to work outside the home, or if you have an additional job inside the home, then hire help. Hired help is worth its weight in gold. It's relatively inexpensive for the amount of peace of mind it provides. (And you could be providing another homeschooled high schooler a job.)

Start house cleaning together when they're young. Get them a cleaning bucket. Head to the dollar store for their rag, scrubs, and cleaning products. Give them jobs to do while you're cleaning.

Use the buddy system. Get the older kids to teach the younger kids. Older kids might love the mentoring job, as they show off their toilet cleaning skills. Assign a younger sibling to an older sibling (greater than a three-year spread, otherwise, you might be managing bickering). Ask the older child to mentor the younger for six months. (This process can also be used in teaching math concepts.)

> If they can do the task, but not perfectly do the task, lower your mama expectations and watch them learn.

Pick chores from a list. You decide what chores need to get done, so you write the list. The kids determine which child does what from the list. Unless they can't agree. Then write those chores on a slip of paper and let them choose from a hat.

Expect you will never be ready for House & Home photographers. Unless you're THAT homeschool mom, in which case we want to see your Insta photos for inspiration. (Or we don't!)

Remember that household activities are covered in the school curriculum, also known as home economics.

Incorporate daily chores in your weekdays. Each child might have their laundry day. (Because they're learning to wash their laundry, rotate their laundry, and fold or hang their laundry at the age you think they are able.) Each week, one child feeds and waters the cats and cleans the litter. Each day, one child empties the dishwasher, and another sweeps the floor. Whatever works in your household?

Fold laundry during read a-louds. Everyone can take turns, even mama. (PS Having kids read aloud helps you assess their reading proficiency, how well they understand new vocabulary, and encourages enunciation.)

Turn on the tunes. Nothing like a little mood music. Find your songs, build a playlist, turn up the tunes, and clean.

Keep a stair basket. No, this is not a new piece of exercise equipment. Place a rectangular basket on the stairs, about three steps up, in which you can put all the kids' stuff that gathers around the house. You know, pieces of Legos or Barbie heads, bits of eraser, and pencils, random socks and ponytails.

Create a kitchen clean-up rotation. Since the dishwasher doesn't work with our hard water, we gave her up. Our youngest, eleven, consistently puts dishes away twice a day, sweeps floors, and wipes counters. (My oldest rolls her eyes because she was five when she started dishwashing). They all learn everything, but at different stages. Everyone knows when they wash or when they dry.

Pay them for chores? This is how I grew up: a quarter for emptying the dishwasher and fifty cents for sweeping the main floor. Rewards might be a motivating tool for your family. I'm a believer we share the house, so we share the work.

Let them earn screen time. Decide the chore, then determine the amount of screen time earned for that chore. Finish shining five windows, and you can have twenty minutes on the screen.

Require them to learn to clean their bedroom. Give kids a list, hang the list behind their door, include the list in your morning chores or your weekend chore list. "Make the bed, put books away, hang up clothes, and place toys on shelves."

Close the door. Accept that kids have messes.

They have a lot going on too. Let them have their space and freedom, barring food that is molding in a bowl on their windowsill.

Rotate the chores. Keep 'em busy, but don't keep 'em bored. Eventually, every chore will become boring. We ALL know that. In the meantime, let them rotate through the list and choose one or two or five activities. You, mama, could also assign the rotation each week.

Beat the timer. The disadvantage of eating a family dinner at home is dishes. Since, all the kids know how to cook and bake. There are a lot of dishes. I'm as motivated as all of them not to do dishes, so let's play a game, let's beat the fifteen-minute timer.

> Your goal is peace of mind in your household. That is all. Not meet your mother-in-law's expectations...

Either do the laundry once a week, ALL day, or a load a day. My youngest has been learning to do his laundry for two years. The older three have been doing their laundry for years before that. Now there's just me and my husband, a load of towels and rags, and the towels/sheets load. Get each child hangers and have them throw the hangers into their laundry baskets on their laundry day so you can teach them to hang them up immediately. Teach folding when they're older.

Good enough is your goal. Pursue perfection, and you'll frustrate yourself. Let it all go, and you'll frustrate yourself. Clean enough to not attract the attention of social services, that is your goal.

Your goal is peace of mind in your household. That is all. Not meet your mother-in-law's expectations, or your cousins', or the Instagram throw pillow extraordinaire. Just think, when they visit you, you're giving your critics something to do.

Back to Marie: spend your extra time holding stuff in your hands and determine if you're going to keep this treasure or if the item has satisfied its life purpose. I'm just going to say, tidy as I am, that I am going to frequently use stuff until it reaches the end of its lifespan (or it gets broken, as this seems like an inevitable end to most of the things I've owned).

My rules for materialistic management:

➢ **Don't bring into my home stuff I don't want.** Even if the item is from someone who desperately wants me to keep that crystal collection.

➤ **Assume someone somewhere wants what I no longer want.** Second-hand store here I come! (But if no one wants that item, the Salvation Army lady has no issue with throwing it away).

➤ **Buy stuff second hand.** Spending a buck on a water glass at a second-hand store is less costly than the three bucks at Walmart. I save two dollars when that item is probably broken in a month anyway.

Once a year, stare each room down and get rid of stuff. Determine if your craft container with embroidery threads and needles really will get used this year. Determine if you will create a day and time when you're getting back to cross stitch after a two-decade hiatus.

Can I make a case against spring cleaning? Just why? Haven't you done enough cleaning all year? When dirt gets uncomfortable enough, you'll find your way to cleaning. Can you accommodate a spider living alongside you and even include that spider in your Charlotte's Web unit study?

Can I make a case for spring cleaning? Some things just can't be done at other times of the year, or are a waste of time, except when done in spring. Take, for example, window cleaning. It rains, it snows. You have clear windows for four months in a year (if you live where I live), so enjoy clarity in the spring. There are some tasks you need to complete annually, like emptying the house vac canister, checking the furnace, filling the propane tank, or checking the gas generator before winter.

You could set aside one week apart to spring clean together. If you have more house than time, just set one week aside. Determine the most important spaces to clean THIS YEAR. Next year will arrive again with new tasks.

> There is no way to be present in everything perpetually when there are too many things to do.

Be Realistic

We orchestrate their education, so we schedule their days with music lessons, schooled subjects, logic games, and prescribed reading. We hope they'll gain understanding, so we discuss the economy, environment, and world politics. We hope they'll gain wisdom, so we guide their sibling and peer interactions. We expect them to take it all in. We expect to keep everything organized. We don't want to miss a beat.

Because we are free from conventional time constraints, we like to fill our empty gaps with more activities. We visit the seniors' center, we visit sick neighbours, and we read charitable request letters with the family to decide on donations. We volunteer in church Sunday schools and youth groups. We plan extensive trips over school scheduled months to adventurous places. A world of interesting people, places, and experiences await us, and we don't want to miss a moment.

We are responsible for our kids' social opportunities, their educational opportunities, their extracurricular opportunities. There's also the mundane housework, groceries, errands, gardens to weed, sidewalks to shovel.

However, there are only so many hours in the day. There is only so much mental space. There is no way to be present in everything perpetually when there are too many things to do.

> ➢ **If there is an opportunity to do something, recognize it comes at the expense of something else.**

> ➢ **Set realistic boundaries with yourself.** Expect yourself not to have a perfect balance ever. Schedule regular checks to make sure you're realistic about your expectations.

➢ **Record how much time activities take**. If you know you want to spend a half-hour with each child discussing their daily activities, then schedule that. If it takes too much time in a day, scatter that activity throughout the week.

➢ **Prioritize your top five activities. Do them first in your day**. Just like many homeschool moms ask kids to begin with math questions because they are the most challenging, get yourself doing your most challenging activity at the beginning of the day.

➢ **Recognize that emotional energy is attached to each activity**. Choose intentionally. Decide what you're going to do with your time and how to invest your emotional energy.

➢ **Unschool your life. Make your life less of a checklist and p**ractice being present and listen to yourself: what do you really want to include in your life?

➢ **Learn about your child's developmental stage.** Is your child capable of your expectations?

➢ **Expect messes.** There will always be pencils and erasers found in couches, science experiments on kitchen counters, dinner plans forgotten (what? you want to eat again?), and attendance at homeschool co-op with dirty sweatpants (that they picked up from the floor yesterday and went to bed in last night).

➢ **Don't expect your kids to have higher grade point averages than schooled kids.** Don't worry when same grade kids learned fractions two years before yours. Kids are just kids. Encourage the actual child in front of you to make the most of who they are.

➢ **Don't expect your kids to take college classes in high school years.** Some kids will not want to attend college ever and some don't want to until they're college age.

➢ **Outsourcing your child's education doesn't mean you're not homeschooling.** Using other resources, like online science teachers, writing programs, or metalwork tutors, training programs, or apprenticeships are useful learning tools too.

➢ **Don't expect your child will understand you the first time.** I've watched my four kids learn (and relearn) times tables over a longer period than I ever expected. Kids process concepts differently than you think.

➢ **Expect to forget an occasional appointment.** Like the chiropractor, a piano lesson, or possibly a child at the piano lesson. Mistakes happen.

➢ **Don't expect your loving children to get along all the time.** I'm like you, I wish this were so; alas, kids fight. Learning to be part of a family is a challenge, learning to interact or not interact, in particular ways.

➢ **Don't expect to create fancy lunches like bento boxes or gourmet organic hot lunches.** You'll have those days where you feel like Suzie Homemaker, but buy protein bars, yoghurt, and bananas for the days you're not.

> ➢ **Just say no.** You can't say yes to everything, even when there's one more cool thing.

> ➢ **Perfect is not realistic.** Good enough is realistic. Practice good enough long enough, and you'll come closer to perfect anyway.

> ➢ **Discuss your expectations with your kids.** Ask them if they think they are reasonable.

> ➢ **Adjust , adjust, adjust.** Don't expect your expectations are ever finely-honed and complete. There's always movement toward learning and growth. (Apparently that's what life is all about, learning and growth.)

> ➢ **Don't expect every day will be fun.** Every day will not, so strike "utopia" from the to-do list.

The Myth of Multitasking

Yes, you are capable. You can text your mother, direct the kids in managing conflict, make dinner, plan evening activities, and show a child where to find the word alliteration in the dictionary. I know you can multitask; you've had lots of practice. But should you?

You can sit between two kids, help one master addition of fractions while assisting the other in learning his cursive letter "P" while you scroll through your online feeds. Is this constant movement how you want to experience your homeschool?

Isn't it enjoyable to work on one thing at a time? To not be thinking about the next thing as you're doing this one thing? Isn't it stressful to respond to more than one person at the same time? One way to be especially mindless and

> Multitasking fuels overwhelm.

unhappy is to insist we do more than a few things at the same time.

Mothers boast about their ability to multitask (I've been one of those moms). We get kids into snow pants while searching for sledding gear, feeding the dog, and folding the last load of laundry at the same time. We might have finished our to-do list, but how did it feel to finish it?

Multitasking fuels overwhelm. Research supports that single tasking (mindful presence in a single activity) is the most satisfying way to approach our work.

Multitasking takes a lot of our working memory and hampers our ability to be creative.

Multitasking became a popular concept back

when marketing PC operating systems were new to the general public: your computer can multitask; you can get so much more done!

A fresh concept for computers back in the day. Probably not all readers will remember when school computer classes offered kids the chance to build a computer program with Logos. Email wasn't a thing. The internet wasn't a thing. The future Facebook inventor wasn't even born yet. Computer technology has changed a lot since my junior high.

I remember hearing a story about the beginning days of the fax machine. People were excited about this technology because fax machines would assist in simplifying people's lives: life would slow down, hours of work would decrease, and overall societal happiness would reign.

I think the only thing multitasking has enabled in our computer technology era is to train us to scan, scan, scan, and not be fully present in activities.

We can explain a math problem to our eight-year-old at the same time we bounce a baby on our lap, then get interrupted by the doorbell, while overhearing a crashing sound in the kitchen. Though these things are demanding our attention, we are mentally planning our afternoon trip to town. We need to go to the grocery store before we bring our daughter to gymnastics and our son to his playdate. We need to buy cat food because we've been relying on canned tuna. After the UPS delivery is received, we head back to the kitchen, but why? Was it to put something on the grocery list? The baby drops her pacifier to the floor; the cat walks over it. "Mom, I just don't get it," our son says as he drops his forehead to his math book. We hear another daughter yell, "Mom, Jennie just dropped an egg on the homeschool floor."

Are we multi-tasking or multi-frustrating ourselves? What you and I both know is you have a lot going on. You're not getting nearly as much done as you are, jangling your nerves, trying to be all things to all people, and doing what you're doing without being there while you do it.

In recent years, the efficiency of multitasking has been debunked. Multitasking is known to decrease productivity. A research study by Meyer, Evans, and Rubinstein say multitasking will decrease productivity by 40 percent. Make your goal doing one activity at a time and engage one child at a time. A 2009 research study from Stanford University discovered that heavy multitaskers were not as capable of sorting important information compared to unimportant details. A 2010 French research study suggested the brain is more likely to make mistakes if we add more than two activities at one time. So instead, prioritize one activity at a time (as much as is reasonably possible). One child at a time. One activity at a time. Do less. Be in the moment.

Practically, that means we're not moving at warp speed. Multitasking doesn't facilitate connections with our kiddos. Kids feel they can't get our attention when we're trying to do too many things. Expect that the kids will have to learn to be more patient and not always have your presence whenever they want our attention. Expect our math-frustrated son has to take a deep breath, ask him politely to wait a minute while we choose to A. answer the door, or B. rescue the egg smash on the floor, or C. ask our daughter to rinse the pacifier. (But not all those activities at once.)

Occupy younger kids when you need focused attention on the older kids. Younger kids demand more attention, typically. There's always a way to occupy toddlers in their highchairs with activities just for this occasion: edible play dough, measuring cups, squirt bottles. Occupy an elementary-aged kid with a documentary or a computer screen while you attend to the youngers (conserve your screen time for this reason). Ask an older child to look after a younger child. Do shorter bursts of activities if you can't maintain everyone's attention in a big chunk.

Focus for fifteen minutes. Instead of constantly switching from one child to another, from one activity to another, devote your full attention to the one activity. Yeah, I know this takes a lot of kid training to let you be separate and do your thing for fifteen whole minutes. Strengthening this muscle, both focusing for fifteen and maintaining kid boundaries, will give you more peace of mind, and you'll get a lot more done.

> **"Say no to many good things, so you can say yes to a few great things."**
>
> **Greg McKeown**

Teresa L. Wiedrick

HOMESCHOOL MAMA COFFEE CHATS

Grab a cup of something hot, coffee or tea, or something cold, a glass of kombucha or an Argentinian Malbec, and let's chat.

Coffee Chat for the First Year Homeschool Mama

Grab a cup of something hot, coffee or tea, or something cold, a glass of kombucha or an Argentinian Malbec, and let's chat.

Let's imagine you have come to my home for a visit near the end of September. The school year is well underway, but we can still enjoy the Adirondack chairs facing the Kootenay River in our front yard.

I'll offer you a mug of hot mint, bergamot, or anise hyssop from my tea garden. We can settle ourselves into the chairs. We'll watch the cedar trees sway and listen to the water rush past the neighbouring island, notice the splash of the beaver jump into the water, and look up to see the geese fly south.

Our kids jump on the trampoline for a solid twenty minutes until they run to the house to get my son's child-sized crossbow to shoot at trees (hopefully, he'll not shoot at the deer or wild turkeys this time). They run around the house a bit, shoes on or off. How they do that on the pea gravel, I do not know. Their activities entertain each other as our Great Pyrenes puppy watches.

Our sixteen chickens cluck towards us in a pack. They notice crumbs from the scones I've offered you. They'll clean it up for us as we chat.

So, let's chat, girlfriend.

So, how have your first few weeks or months of this homeschool thing been? It's been quite the memorable first few weeks of your year homeschool.

I know you're excited that you've discovered this amazing new lifestyle. And you are right, it is fantastic in so many ways. Freedom to schedule as you wish. Freedom from schedules if you prefer. Freedom to choose curriculum or no curriculum. Freedom to follow your children's passions. Freedom to follow your passions too. Freedom to not wake up at the crack of dawn, or to wake up at the crack of dawn before the kids wake. Freedom to not have to buy indoor shoes. Freedom to not check homework or sign field trip release forms. Freedom to do extracurriculars in the middle of the day and do errands too.

You're enamored with homeschooling. I'm so happy for you.

May I make four suggestions that will help you continue enjoying homeschooling?

➤ **Don't overschedule.** If your first foray into homeschool planning includes reading homeschool philosophy books like Charlotte Mason, classical homeschooling, or project-based homeschooling, you may have created a schedule that might overwhelm a trained schoolteacher. Homeschool planning books will offer many things to explore, so read and plan. But recognize what many long-term homeschoolers have learned; you'll burn yourself out trying to include every clever activity. As a result of that burnout, you'll wonder if you've made a terrible, terrible mistake homeschooling in the first place. Build margins into your days so you can have downtime. Have fun with your kids and follow your kids' interests. You'll build your philosophy as time goes by.

➢ **Don't over-purchase.** You could go into a homeschool convention "just to look," but I'll bet in the first year you probably won't. Bring luggage, they say (for all the books and curriculum you're about to purchase). I say, in your excitement to plan your children's education, you might spend a mortgage payment in your first year. By your tenth year, you'll still be using the unused curriculum. Or you can buy a little curriculum and supplement with a library card. Think "the library is my homeschool curriculum" (then supplement as needed). I know you need books. I am aware you feel the pressure to have every book for every conceivable knowledge thread at your fingertips. I have five full bookshelves for just that purpose. The internet and library can be your bookshelves too.

> **Don't over-plan.** Come August, and most homeschool mamas are hankering to plan another year of activities. That's what happens after a relaxing summer. Because kids aren't as appreciative of the planned, scripted days you prepared for them, they won't always thank you that their every moment has a plan. All your efforts might make your existence feel validated, but your kids aren't invested in completing your to-do list. Write your ideas in a planning journal, then hold them loosely and go with the flow.

> All your efforts might make you feel validated, but your kids aren't invested in completing your to-do list.

True: your kids' education requires conscientiousness. Why do this whole thing if we're not going to do it right? Bigger question: what is "right"? We're not competing with Google and we're not trying to replace God as we educate our children. We're trying to equip individuals to develop in their unique ways so they can grow up to become the unique people and contributors they were meant to be.

Don't expect too much. Of yourself or your kids. We hope to enjoy every moment with our children, love every activity we've planned, read every book we've purchased, and plan specific activities for every subject. This is the mathematical formula for homeschool frustration and unhappiness. These homeschool responsibilities come with great rewards, but a great reward comes with great effort. There is a reason the public's eyes bug out when you share you're a homeschool family. Their gut instinct, that homeschooling is hard work, that it may be an overwhelming responsibility, is correct. There are few breaks. No external rewards. No pay. Often few accolades. (Once, I was told I made up a job that didn't need to exist. Nice. Thanks for that.) There is a small circle that even acknowledges your efforts, so you'd better be telling yourself you're doing a great job and don't be unrealistic with your mama heart.

Now that I've warned you before you're too far along, know that you will do all these things. Your concerned neighbours, friends, family, and random strangers await your response: How does homeschool work? What is your daily plan? How will the kids be socialized? Will you educate them "right"?

I'll tell you why you shouldn't overschedule, over purchase, over plan, and expect much: it will drain your happiness. **Make your goal family happiness.** Happiness happens, and then happiness passes too. But we're all wired for happiness, whether we like to tell ourselves that or not. Real-life, real living, with all the challenges and curveballs, knocks at everyone's door. That's life. I'm confident anyone that anyone who entered the homeschool world has a certain level of idealism and optimism. Expect you're going to expect too much. Be gracious with yourself when you discover you're there. And focus on the happiness of you and your family.

Coffee Chat for the Established Homeschool Mama

You've learned about every curriculum under the sun. You even could write your own homeschool book. You've bought all the books: the read aloud books, the math textbooks, the science and history books, the how-to homeschool books, the encouraging mama homeschool books hopefully, the guide to homeschool philosophy books, and the homeschool curriculum recommendation books.

You've soaked up every blog, subscribed to

every homeschool podcast, joined every Instagram homeschool account, and Facebook homeschool thread. You've even started a blog and pinned to your own homeschool Pinterest boards.

You've heard it all. You've sampled it all. Your kids have been the guinea pigs. You might have graduated a kid, or two, or six. You've learned a lot about learning and a lot about kids.

You can write a paragraph on each of the homeschool philosophies. You've tried them all. Now you're a self-described eclectic, because if you give a homeschool family time, we all become eclectic. We're all taking a little bit of this and a little bit of that, whether it's parenting advice, curriculum suggestions, or menu plans. You are not representations of any philosophy. You do things the way you do them because your way works for you and your family.

You've tried all the parenting expertise, homeschool expertise, and household management expertise. You've learned they all work, but they only work some of the time and then you do things your way.

You've seriously considered sending the kids to school at different times or you've left the house in such a disaster you subconsciously hoped the social worker would show up to take the kids away (but just for the weekend). There have been days that were overwhelming and frustrating; time away would have been most welcome.

The kids might have fought over the green cup too many times, but you've also had a few mini breakdowns because another glass got broken or someone fidgeted during math time. Perhaps it was that time you had enough of the kids sassingarguingwhiningcomplaining. There was the time you had a panic attack when you first entertained homeschooling high school. There was the time your partner was out of work, and you had to return to work, but you kept the kids homeschooling. There was the time you had a challenging pregnancy or post-partum periods with colicky, non-sleeping babies, or chronic illness. There was the time you decided to separate for the good of the children. Hopefully, not all these events happened in your family. We all have some of those times.

> You've got a book to share, a resource you love, so share the love, and share your knowledge.

These are the reasons you know you're a veteran homeschooler, an expert, or at the very least, have something to share with new homeschoolers.

You've learned how to function as a homeschooler under so many circumstances. **So, please share your expertise.** Be the mentor. You've got a book to share, a resource you love, so share the love, and share your knowledge. For every seasoned homeschool mama, there are nine new homeschoolers. (Not a confirmed statistic, just a guess based on a lot of new homeschool bloggers that talk about their new homeschool lives and that's just the homeschoolers that blog their homeschool world.) However, just because people start homeschooling doesn't mean they will continue homeschooling.

Have a homeschool moms coffee time while kids hang out. Meeting new homeschoolers is fun. (Spoken by an extrovert). Introduce yourself, share with others how many years you've been homeschooling, a little about your kids, and be open to sharing your thoughts on academics and socialization, about the good, the bad, the in-between, the freedoms, the restrictions. Mostly, listen to these brave women share their struggles, their challenges, and their exciting plans for their families.

Share with non-homeschool groups about

homeschooling. Share your expertise with local preschool moms' groups. Why not share the freedom before the families even consider what educational path their child might take? If you can't find a group of homeschool women nearby, I guarantee you will find one on-line. Homeschool Facebook groups abound.

Hold a coffee meeting or family playground visit for new homeschool moms with questions. Introduce yourself, then ask them what questions they have. Serve hot drinks, ask your older kids to entertain the younger kids, and that is all you need. These folks will be most grateful to chat with other homeschool parents.

> What are you going to do after you've graduated from homeschooling? Develop who you are before the kids leave.

Serve on provincial or state homeschool boards. I write the newsletter for our provincial homeschool board. As a strong proponent of freedom and family-led home education, I want to do everything I can to encourage and support our homeschool freedoms. Even if you merely subscribe to a local homeschool advocacy group, there is strength in representative numbers.

Develop lectures and seminars. (Okay, stop the bus, now I've gone too far). You, yes, you, have more expertise than any new homeschool mama. If you can get through a year or two and you're still committed to homeschool, you're in the established homeschoolers group. You have knowledge and wisdom you don't even know you have until you talk to someone who is just beginning. Share what you know with your world.

And final thoughts, don't get lost in the homeschool mama identity.

You'll have yourself after the kids are all gone. So, who are you? You won't always be a homeschool mama. What are you going to do after you've graduated from homeschooling? Develop who you are before the kids leave.

But aren't you glad you've invested your energy and efforts in your family? What a story you've written — ebbs and flow, joys and heartbreaks, lessons in learning about learning, life and love. We established homeschool mamas see your efforts and declare to one another: well done, mama! It was worth every gray hair, every heated moment, and every fairytale memory for the storybook of our family's lives.

Well done, mama! You've turned your challenges into your charms.

Coffee Chat for the Tired Homeschooler

There comes a time in the homeschool life that mama gets tired of homeschooling. This seems hard to believe in the beginning homeschool fervor. But this doesn't seem so hard to consider when a mama has been around a few years.

It was September, and I had spent the month busying myself canning, organizing the house, and reading about homeschooling because I was anticipating the onslaught of household neglect when studies started again.

I was spent.

Curiously, I just wanted to sit and stare out the Great Room window, watch the downtown traffic scurry by, and the pedestrians pass the stone wall of our front yard.

I wanted a nap, even a week of naps. I tried to cozy up in my bed in the middle of the day and sleep. This was unlike me.

Could I schedule a week of no schedule? Do nothing? Am I even capable of doing nothing? I wanted no devotions with breakfast, no afternoon history reading, no prescribed quiet time, and no bedtime reading.

Had I ever done that? To everything there is a season. Perhaps I could take a short season of rest.

Perhaps I was tired because I maintained summer schooling throughout the year. We started early July the first year and went all year through. All four kids began their first day of school in their summer dresses and flip flops. I was eager to begin!

My kids loved learning, I was eager to start, and I wasn't compelled to follow a school routine, so I went through the summer. But, girlfriend, I needed a break! I might have prevented fatigue if I had learned to go to the bookstore, buy cheesy, easy summer novels with colourful covers, the ones you would never put on your kids' reading list, then find a watering hole near you, pack a bag with swimsuits and towels, pack snacks, and head to the beach. Play. Dip those toes and read under the giant umbrella. Find your summertime splendor: no schedule, no cares.

By February of the third or fourth year, I was very, very tired. I've learned that February is a common month for homeschool burnout. Every February I hear moms complain of boredom and fatigue, the slump month. As excited as they are about their new fall study plans, excitement always wanes, and unschooling, or child-directed activities, seem like the best choice by February.

Find me something to do that isn't what we've already been doing! Make me an interesting schedule. Make it not come out of a workbook. Make me not hear my voice over and over as I read another read aloud.

May feels like the natural end of the formal study year because May is warm and sunny where I live. The garden needs to be planted; botany becomes my unschooled focus. People need to swing the back door open and shut a few dozen times a day. That door has not had enough exercise over winter.

> When the kids are grinding out work, what are they absorbing?

Might I suggest choosing a shift in rhythm to offset seasonal fatigue? There are lots of home economics opportunities when we tire of routines. Some people call it spring cleaning. Some people also call it the same thing school kids do the last week before summer break: kids tidy their desks, wash cupboards, organize pencils, books, and supplies. Homeschooled kids do spring cleaning inside their family home instead.

If you're lucky, you take the show on the road in frazzled, fed-up February. Vacation to a sunny, idyllic destination, and don't bring the workbooks. Cabin fever forces indoor time, which facilitates contemplation about what we're doing. Sometimes it's useful to slow down.

May I suggest doing nothing? Just for a day or two? Think anti-Nike: just don't do it! When the kids are grinding out work, what are they absorbing? Whatever it takes to get the vigor back, even stopping altogether, do that.

Change the routine. I've learned to stop the original routine when I get bored. If I'm bored, so are my kids. Therefore, we delete the boring stuff. Instead of finishing all the Simply Grammar lessons, we put away the discussions on antecedents and indeterminate pronouns for next September (if even the writer in me doesn't care, is it valuable)? Maybe we'll do math one day, but not necessarily the next. When we're bored, we change the routine.

Get realistic. Busy Moms Survival Guide podcast host, PJ Jonas, had much to say about exceeding mama's unrealistic expectations. She spoke of requiring margins in her daily schedule. Give yourself plenty of time to get places, don't overschedule, plan personal time and date nights. Give yourself margins.

Until I began scheduling my daily activities in my iPod, I had no idea how unrealistic I was. I simply wasn't getting my to-do list completed. When I scheduled all my intended activities into a Day Timer, I discovered that coordinating four hours of studies for four kiddos, making three meals, keeping the laundry machines busy, and completing additional housework, was hard to accomplish in a single day. Yet, this wasn't all I intended to do! I also expected to work on three writing projects, write three blog posts that week, finish a Shutterfly photo book, scrapbook each child's year, and hopefully, start any craft I'd pinned ever.

As I painstakingly audited all my activities, I discovered I was a wee bit unrealistic. Besides that, I expected I should be present, not planning the next ten things on my list for the next day, or the next month. I began to schedule margins of quiet time into my day and accept reality: I couldn't do everything because everything I was doing made me tired.

The season of homeschool fatigue happens to every one of us. We shouldn't run a homeschool co-op if we have five kids under six. We probably shouldn't insist our kids carry a full academic load when we've just had a baby (or if we do, we're going to be doing those activities on the couch as we nurse the baby while the kids move back and forth between their books and snacks.) No child will implode if we change things up or do less.

Coffee Chat for Stressful Times

When the stress gets more intense, some of us collapse onto sofas and some of us force forward. No matter how you deal with challenges like unexpected illnesses, relationship separations, family deaths, unemployment loss, or pandemics, there's no question mixing that these scenarios with a homeschool routine makes for a lot of stress.

> I'll say it on repeat...there is no academic emergency. Your well-being and the well-being of your family is the most important thing.

Let the kids know how you're feeling or how you're dealing with the stress. Make sure to ask them about how they're feeling too. You don't have to inappropriately share details or rely on their support to let them know how you're doing. One thing they do subconsciously (or consciously) know is how their parents are coping. Homeschooled kids know a lot about their homeschool parents.

Make memories. Accept that life is going to throw you some unexpected curveballs, then decide to play ball on the fly. Mix up your day and make memories so you will remember that time as bittersweet, not just bitter. Play every game in the house when a pandemic rolls into town. Create new family traditions when a partner leaves the home. Create family grieving rituals when a special someone passes on.

Expect unreliable, rollercoaster emotions to interrupt your day. Plan for these times. Get outside help, whether it's for emotional coping or cleaning the kitchen.

Expect that you won't always know what to do. Talk to someone. If you don't have someone you can share your real feelings with, find someone whom you can pay to do that.

Consider a season of sending the kids to school. If your coping skills have turned into laying on the sofa midday because of chronic illness or depression, and if you're unsure where the kids are, you might consider that you're no longer up to the homeschool scenario. You don't have to assume you're leaving it permanently. Perhaps a season of the kids leaving to school each day and returning in the afternoon will provide you rest and reprieve long enough to gather perspective, so you'll want to homeschool.

Lower the expectations. I'll say it on repeat, over and over and over, there is no academic emergency. Your well-being and the well-being of your family is the most important thing. Every single time. Don't let an academic schedule become the focus when you're feeling the challenge of stressful times.

> "We can do no great things, only small things with great love."

> **Mother Teresa**

Choosing Your Purpose

One of the most important things you can do for yourself is to have a clear purpose, not just in your homeschool world, but in your entire life.

Once upon a time we sold our custom-built home, moved provinces and professions, significantly decreased responsibility in that profession, and decided to homeschool instead of private school. In all this, we made a dramatic shift towards simplicity. We bought a home that had character, which didn't entirely reflect my style, but housed our essential belongings while we spent half our time traveling.

My goal was simplicity. I wanted to throw off anything that would keep me from feeling like I was living life on purpose.

Travelling certainly encourages simple living. It's much easier being in the moment when there is nothing else to do but soak up new things to see and do and learn in a novel location. There's no laundry piling up because you only brought a tiny part of your wardrobe. There aren't many belongings to look after, floors to wash, or meals to prep. I remember saying to my husband twice during our travels, once in Venice and once in the rural mountains of Kenya, we should sell everything, live off the proceeds, and volunteer our time until we run out of money. A lack of clean water, consistent electricity, and irregular food availability kept me from selling everything and traveling to the developing world. (Malaria and Ebola also deterred me, but those stories are for a different book.)

Somewhere during those seven years, I became fascinated with the idea of homesteading off-grid, living an hour away from town in a 500 square foot cabin. Luckily, my husband projected into the future and reminded me we would have three teenage girls and a pre-adolescent boy. Enough said.

I learned that getting rid of my dream home, my U2 Joshua Tree cassette tape, my yoghurt maker, and any other belongings I gave away, didn't translate to a more purposeful life. I learned that traveling to foreign lands, both exotic (northeastern Ghana or rural Kenya) and charming (Italy, the Netherlands, Belgium and France), even travelling to the ends of the earth (right up to the Beaufort Sea), did not translate into a more purposeful life either. *I learned it wasn't simplicity I was after; I was searching for focus and purpose.*

You can spend less, buy less, and organize more, but you won't find an internal sense of purpose. I've tried that and come out the other side. Now I miss my Joshua Tree cassette tape and my yoghurt maker. With an intent to downsize, simplify my life, and decrease clutter, I gave away parts of me.

The difference between simplicity and purpose: a fine line, really. If you have a collection of cheese boards and cheese knives, and a pantry of bottled wines, I assume you like wine and cheese nights. If you're only collecting those things, because they sound like items that reflect the kind of person you'd like to be, then maybe you need to simplify. Let someone have them that enjoys them. If those things reflect you, why give them up?

Simplifying your life is not so much about anti-materialistic efforts as it is about focusing our attention on activities that are meaningful and purposeful to us.

How to find your purpose?

Determine your life values. Choose one word

or three that summarize your most important values. Each year I choose three different words. This year I've chosen the words: expansion, encourage, and invite. (If you want to learn why, you'll have to come for coffee). These value words remind us how we want to focus our intentions and how we want to spend each of our days. Determine how to engage those values practically, moment by moment during your day. Doing this makes your daily goals focused and purposeful.

Write these chosen value words in your journal each morning. Practice these words as you live. Share those words with your kids. Occasionally check to see that your activities and your relationships reflect those values. Live into your values and you'll find your purpose.

Choose a Theme Song. Play it in the car. Play it before your morning read aloud. Remind others and remind yourself what you're all about.

Sarah Susanka, in her book, *The Not So Big Life: Making Room for What Really Matters*, compares the not so big life with the remodeling of a house, which certainly has relevance to me as I've designed and built homes. Here is the list of her book's chapter titles (used with permission):

Blueprint for a new way of living-

Noticing what inspires you

Identifying what isn't working

Removing the clutter

Listening to your dreams

Learning to see through the obstacles

Improving the quality of what you have

Creating a place and time of your own

Proceeding through the construction process

Moving into your not-so-big-life

Maintaining your newly remodeled life

Being at home in your life

Susanka reminds us: "A life that's well-composed is one in which there is authenticity all the way through, a life in which the outer appearance and the inner substance match up."

Taking Stock

You are a homeschool mama now, but you won't always be. One day you weren't a mom, and then your first child was born or adopted. One day the youngest will graduate, begin his journey away from your home, and then the homeschool mama identity you have will no longer be a full-time job.

Take stock to determine if you are intentionally doing the things you want to do with your life. Once a year, spend time with your journal and consider the following questions excerpted from The Year End Review Exercise from Chapter 11 of *The Not So Big Life* by Sarah Susanka:

- ➢ How have I spent my time?
- ➢ What are the results of the actions I have taken?
- ➢ What events, realizations, and understanding have come into being?
- ➢ What has inspired me?
- ➢ What makes me grateful?
- ➢ What were my sorrows and disappointments, and how have they changed me?
- ➢ What books have I read this year and what impact have they had?

- ➤ What movies and other entertainments have moved me, and in what ways?
- ➤ What journeys have I taken?
- ➤ What conditioned patterns have I recognized, and what experiences have allowed me to see them more clearly?

Then engage questions about your present:

- ➤ How am I different now from the way I was last year at this time?
- ➤ How can I integrate the critical lessons of the past year into my life?
- ➤ Are there any strategies, phrases, or questions that have significance for me right now?
- ➤ Are there any things I'm trying to force into existence right now? If so, what would happen if I stopped trying to make them happen?
- ➤ To what part of myself am I giving birth?
- ➤ What am I becoming?
- ➤ Has my experience of time changed at all since last year?

Then engage questions about your future:

- ➤ What is it I wish to focus on or experience in the coming year?
- ➤ If I could sum up all my desires and longings in a straightforward statement

spoken from the highest aspect of myself, what would it be?

Take stock, so you can determine your daily purpose. Perhaps in taking stock we will come to understand that the struggle and striving and all the busyness is not our purpose, but that meaning can be found in simply being present in the moments.

"When you make the time and the space
for what you long to do,
the world around you will shift in all
sorts of apparently miraculous ways
to support the realization of that
longing."
-Sarah Susanka, *The Not So Big Life*

A Final Letter to you, Mama

Once upon a time, you likely told yourself you have one of the best jobs in the world. You took on this job, and no one expected you to.

You get to watch your kids grow up right before your eyes. You get to watch them learn chess moves at three, win chess games with dad at eight, and create their own Minecraft servers. You get to see their vivacious, animated personality create a successful YouTube channel. You get to watch their fascination with dolphins turn into aquatic on-line science classes then into medical school applications. You get to observe their people-watching passions turn into a social sciences degree, watch their preoccupation with history reading on their bed turn into a Greek and Latin Civ History minor. You get to see them develop their interests as they grow into adulthood.

You get to develop your interests too. If you're interested in Greek mythology, you can buy a book, read the book with your kids, take courses online, build Greek columns from sugar cubes, wrap yourself in white sheets, make a crown of grape leaves and have your kids feed you grapes, olives and wine on the living room floor, and call that Social Studies. You get to dabble in your interests, just like you encourage your kids to dabble in theirs. You get to start home businesses, start Etsy shops, create a work life around your homeschool, or a homeschool around your work life.

You get to do the homeschool hygge. Isn't it funny how outsiders think we're tethered to all things uncomfortable; meanwhile, we steadily move toward all things hygge? Do they not know we can choose to let the kids sleep in if they want? Do they know we don't feel pressured toward cultural trends, nor do we even know about them a lot of the time? Do they not know we get to move at the flow of our family, and we influence the flow of our family to fit our needs too? We get chocolate chip cookies with math workbooks, family room fires with afternoon reading, tea and essential oils throughout school days, and candlelight, just because.

Mama, has anyone told you that you have one of the best jobs in the world?

Homeschooling can be a challenge to maintain mama's self-care, but the homeschool lifestyle can also be a charmed life that encourages mama's self-care.

It's a challenge to build your needs, your wants and your personality into your homeschool world, but it can be done, and it will be done as you continue moving forward, instilling habits and practices that take care of you.

So, let's keep working towards turning our challenges into our *charms*. I wish you and your family health and happiness as you learn to go beyond survival to thriving as you nurture the nurturer.

Teresa L. Wiedrick

Teresa offers coaching for homeschool mamas and is available for speaking engagements. You can get in touch with her at

www.capturingthecharmedlife.com

For self-care stories and inspiration, listen to her podcast, *Homeschool Mama Self Care*.